371.94 HAR

D1352782

1806408

AUTISM
<u>AND</u> ICT

UNIVERSITY OF WALES COLLEGE NEWPORT
LIBRARY AND LEARNING RESOURCES CAERLEON

371.94 HAR

AUTISM AND ICT

A GUIDE FOR TEACHERS & PARENTS

Colin Hardy, Jan Ogden,
Julie Newman and Sally Cooper

David Fulton Publishers

London

David Fulton Publishers Ltd
Ormond House, 26–27 Boswell Street, London WC1N 3JZ

www.fultonpublishers.co.uk

First published in Great Britain by David Fulton Publishers in 2002

Note: The rights of Colin Hardy, Jan Ogden, Julie Newman and Sally Cooper to be identified as the authors of this work have been asserted by them in accordance with the Copyright, Designs and Patents Act 1988.

Copyright © 2002 Colin Hardy, Jan Ogden, Julie Newman and Sally Cooper

British Library Cataloguing in Publication Data
A catalogue record for this book is available from the British Library.

ISBN 1–85346–824–X

Except for those pages that carry a copyright line, which may be photocopied for use only within the purchasing institution, all rights reserved. No part of this publication may be reproduced, stored in a retrieval system or transmitted, in any form, or by any means, electronic, mechanical, photocopying, recording or otherwise, without the prior permission of the publisher.

Typeset by Keyset Composition, Colchester, Essex
Printed and bound in Great Britain by Bell and Bain Ltd, Glasgow

Contents

|\||

Acknowledgements

We would like to thank the following people who kindly read through the first draft of this book and gave us their comments: Jane May (Teacher in Charge of the Tollgate Enhanced Provision, LBN), Alison Orphan (parent of a child with autistic spectrum disorders), Shirley Dinig (mother of one of the authors, Julie Newman), John Newman (Julie's husband) and Pam Wright (Training Manager, Inclusive Education Team, LBN). Our thanks go to Des Rodrigues (Technician, Learning Support Development and Advisory Service, LBN) for his advice on technical aspects in the book.

In addition we thank Linda Amber, and her son Paul, for their thoughts and ideas.

We are grateful to Trish Hornsey of Inclusive Technology Ltd for granting permission to use a number of images from their catalogue and in particular our thanks to Dave Hornsey for his work converting these images to print quality.

Some of the images in Chapter 4 are protected by US and worldwide copyrights, and are owned by Media Graphics International, Inc.

1 Introduction

The allure of computers

In the course of writing this book we spoke to a large number of people who knew a child on the autistic spectrum: parents, carers, learning support assistants, teachers and so on. What was striking about these conversations was that, in virtually all cases, mention of the word *computer* unleashed positive, enthusiastic and, in some cases, amusing anecdotes about their child.

Two or three common themes were repeated time and time again, most important of which was the simple fact that children with autism like computers. Typical were the comments of the grandparent of a child with Asperger's syndrome (age six), who often found herself in the role of carer while her son was at work:

> He absolutely adores computers, it's the thing he goes straight to in his class and it's the thing he goes to when he is frustrated.
>
> He may have played with his father's PC at home before. He comes downstairs to my computer, switches it on, goes through all the procedures, uses the CD to load programs and uses the mouse. I do not think that he was taught this but just watched others. He does not mind sitting and watching others on the computer. For example he saw this racing program and then the next time on the computer he loaded it up by himself and started playing.
>
> He also loves his tape recorder; he puts the tapes in and listens by himself. He likes videos and will load them himself, often will pause the video and rewind and re-watch one sequence again and again.

The comments about the ease and relative speed with which computer routines could be learnt were oft repeated. This from the support teacher of a year six (ten years old) pupil at a mainstream primary school:

> She loved the computer. She was really good on it. She could do anything once they told her what to do. She could do it herself the next time. She could learn a set of rules and she knew that these would not change so she could keep adding to her knowledge.

And similarly from a support teacher of a pupil in year two reception:

> It seemed as though he had spent most of his second year in reception screaming. He had no spoken language, just some sounds and vocalization. Suddenly it seemed he noticed the computer, I thought that I would have to get him a tracker ball or joystick but within three days he had mastered the mouse. He was totally involved with the programs, making choices and loading programs, all within three days.
>
> His Learning Support Assistant (LSA) would only need to show him things once then he could do it.

Another surprising but common theme was the computer as a catalyst for social interaction. An infant school teacher made the following comments about a child with autism in her class:

He becomes animated on the computer and more than that he will actually converse with the child next to him. He lets them use the mouse and he will talk to them telling them which buttons to press and what to do. This is the child who normally hardly ever talks to any child and finds it hard to form any words. The computer is a stimulus to language for him.

Often closely tied in with this social aspect are descriptions of a 'child helper' whose technical skills and ability to fix computer problems is a refreshing antidote to failure in other areas of the curriculum. Success on the computer can be a real boost to self-esteem and a means to enhance credibility amongst fellow pupils. The following is from a support teacher of a child who was then in year six (ten years old):

Computers, he loved them, to the extent that he could be walking past a classroom and he would hear the computer and be able to name what type it was from the buzz and hum that he could hear.

He wasn't too much into using commercial software but he loved the technical side of it. He was a wizard at changing the set-up, the speed of the mouse, and so on. He enjoyed tricking the other pupils, inviting them to play a game, then setting the level too hard for them and watching their reaction! But he soon got a reputation for being the person who could 'fix' the computer and used this to his advantage as a means to avoid work!

It gave him a lot of credibility in class. This proved very important given the competitive nature of Asperger's syndrome. He also had dyspraxia, and very poor handwriting, and was clearly a poor performer in conventional academic subjects.

The obsession with computers had amusing results in the case of the next child:

I worked with him in year six and, because I knew how much he liked computers, I tried my best, unsuccessfully, to get him a laptop. I didn't see him again until I visited his secondary school some two to three years later. He ran up to me when he saw me walking across the playground. I expected a warm greeting. But, no, his only words were 'Miss you still haven't got me the laptop'!

If you want to add a bit of objectivity to this rough and ready survey try it for yourself; ask someone you know who has autism, or a carer, teacher or support worker, what they feel about information and communication technology (ICT)?

Practical task

Ask a parent, carer, or teacher of a child with autism 'How does your child feel about computers?'

Better still ask the children themselves.

It is clear to us that information and communication technology has a special appeal to children on the autistic spectrum. We would not suggest that all children with autistic spectrum disorders (ASD) like computers, although the rare negative examples that we have come across can sometimes be traced back to inappropriate or stressful approaches to ICT use with the child (Chapter 6 of this book suggests ways to avoid this unfortunate circumstance).

We would also not wish to portray ICT as an alternative or competing medium to more conventional or 'low tech' approaches, but would see ICT as complementing and building on these.

How this book is set out

- By the end of this opening chapter we hope that, if you are not already convinced of the usefulness of ICT for children with autism, you will have heard enough to persuade you to investigate further.
- By the end of Chapters 2–3 we hope that you will have a clearer idea of what autism is and what this 'looks like in the classroom' in terms of pupil performance and behaviour. Chapter 3 concludes with a simple profile format to help you focus in on an individual child and identify which elements of autism are significant.
- By the end of Chapter 4 we hope that you have a clear picture of what ICT is. More importantly we define qualities of ICT and suggest how these may, in varying degrees, address different aspects of autism. Chapter 4 concludes with a simple star diagram to help you define for an individual child which qualities of ICT are most likely to be relevant.
- Chapters 1–4 taken together attempt to solve a dilemma. In a book that looks at two themes, in this case autism and also ICT, how much time do you spend on each and how do you bring them together? We hope that these chapters offer you a rationale to achieve this. The autism profile at the end of Chapter 3 and the ICT star diagram at the end of Chapter 4 are intended as summaries to help you hold both perspectives in mind when considering the needs of a specific child.
- This rationale is brought to life in Chapter 5 in the form of a range of 'case studies' of real children, but with fictitious names, describing how ICT has been used. We hope that in this chapter you will find at least one 'real life' example that compares to a child whom you know or work with.
- By Chapter 6 you may well be wanting to try out some of these ideas with a child. So we begin with dos and don'ts associated with early computer use for children with autism. In Chapters 6 and 7 we look at two major areas of concern in relation to school: communication, and writing and recording.
- Chapter 8 explores another common area of interest, the Internet.
- By Chapter 9, we assume that you must be enthusiastic to have read this far! So you may be thinking about buying or expanding your own computer. By the end of this chapter we hope you will have a better idea of what to look for and how to get started.
- By the end of Chapter 10 we hope that you have some ideas of how to carry your interest in ICT and autism forward.

Reference will be made to the National Curriculum for England (QCA/DfEE 1999). Bearing in mind the broader readership of this book, wherever possible, this will be done in a context to give a more general insight into how ICT can be taught and exploited in a school context to reduce barriers to learning for pupils with autism.

Wherever possible we have offered photocopyable checklists and charts to help you focus and structure the information we offer in relation to the needs of a specific child with autism.

A small group of parents and teachers were kind enough to read through this manuscript in its draft form and offer us advice on its content and layout. Some read it as a whole; others dipped in and out of chapters according to their interest. Whichever way you read it we hope you will find something of value and interest and will feel more confident to experiment with ICT, along with the children.

2 What is autism?

The key to autism is the key to the nature of human life. (Wing 1996, p. 225)

Within this chapter we will be exploring aspects of behaviour, learning and communication, which combine to define ASD (autistic spectrum disorders). Many authors have previously written in depth about this subject and we will be outlining the main theories; yet there will not be space enough to give justice to this field of study. Therefore, we will give an extensive reference list in order for interested parents/carers and colleagues to pursue their own investigations.

The most worthwhile method, however, of discovering what ASD means to individuals and those closely involved with their well-being is to be with them: exist closely with them, share their lives and gain experience of their personality, preferred learning styles and interests. Theories alone will not be beneficial; therefore what follows are two brief case studies, which outline real strengths and difficulties in order to bring the theories to life.

Andrew

Andrew has a diagnosis of ASD and severe learning difficulties. He attends a mainstream school in an inclusive London Borough. He has attended the same school since starting in the Nursery. He enjoyed water play and spent a lot of time flitting from one activity to another seemingly oblivious to the presence of his peers, but apparently quite happy. His behaviour changed when he transferred into the main school building at the beginning of his Reception year.

He spent nearly all day screaming and trying to escape from the classroom, unless he was left on his own to wander around the classroom and to pick up anything that caught his interest, even for a brief moment of time. If another child was holding what he wanted, he would take it from their grasp. If they resisted, he would scream and try to hit or bite them. Andrew tended to be passionate in his desire to hold one particular thing, such as a plastic farm animal, for a period of a few days. If an adult tried to direct his attention he would scream, cover his ears and attempt to leave the classroom. He communicated with adults by pulling at their sleeves or screaming. The screams would continue until the adult with him distracted him or happened, with the aid of good guesswork, to give him what he wanted.

He was unaware of the other members of his class and the class routine. He was not toilet trained.

When the sun shone and he was outside in the playground he would cover his eyes. His parents provided him with a baseball cap, which he would wear, pulled down over his eyes, whenever the light was bright, whether inside or outside.

He was also sensitive to certain noises, particularly when inside. If the children were singing a song he would cover his ears and scream. He could not attend assembly, as all sounds in the hall would have the same effect on him as the children singing. Yet when he walked through the empty hall he would shout and make noises with apparent enjoyment.

At home he would exhibit similar behaviour to that at school. When his mother took him home after school he would scream and cry until she took him out in his buggy for about an hour and a half. At home he wandered around the house.

Gradually he started to become used to the school environment and routines and the frequency of screaming reduced. His support assistant learned to understand what his various screams meant.

Towards the end of his Reception year he noticed the computer. He started to watch his peers working on the computer and it was observed that, when he started to become distressed, he would go to the computer and become calmer. In Year 1 he sat down in front of it and started to try to use the 'mouse'. Within an hour he had mastered control of the mouse. From this point onwards he quickly learned to change programs, repeat parts of programs that he preferred (mainly cause and effect programs) and he started to respond verbally to the computer. Previously he had uttered one or two words, but with the computer he would repeat the sounds of letters on a simple literacy program. He transferred this new-found knowledge to other literacy work in the classroom. His length of concentration increased dramatically from one or two minutes to fifteen minutes. Soon he started to transfer his ability to concentrate when working on the computer to other activities in the classroom. He also started to transfer some of the knowledge he was gaining from the computer to his differentiated curriculum. The adult who supported him 100 per cent during the day began to sit beside him and share the computer with him. At first he resisted but now he will work cooperatively with not only an adult but also a peer. He is more aware of his peers, no longer screams, will participate in the whole school curriculum, is toilet trained in school and although he is still functioning at a basic level he rarely becomes upset in school and is making slow but steady progress. Obviously this change in behaviour is not totally due to the 'magic' of the computer but Andrew's attraction to it has meant that the adults working with him have a way to get to know him better.

His parents have a computer at home now. He will happily sit there and work on various programs. The days of cold walks pushing the buggy round the streets are over!

Rashid

When I first encountered Rashid he was a year three pupil in a resourced unit attached to a mainstream primary school. His previous school career had led him into a unit for pupils with emotional and behavioural difficulties. He had a great deal of negative experiences before a paediatrician had given a diagnosis of Asperger's syndrome.

Rashid was a very anxious child who had an extensive vocabulary and could indeed talk at length about interests such as Super Mario Brothers or golf. His reading age was well above his chronological age yet he would have difficulty with comprehending more abstract meanings embedded within the text. He excelled at mathematics and could run through complex calculations mentally. Rashid would get very annoyed when teachers would ask him to present his 'workings out' because he found it difficult to explain the process, and anyway 'What was the point?'

Socially, Rashid would be driven toward adult interaction. Adults would be more tolerant of him and listen to his favourite interests (well for a while anyway). However he found the area of peer interaction a minefield. He could not understand why they would not always do what he wanted to do, he would not listen to their ideas and thoughts and he found team activities both within the classroom setting and out of the formal settings very frustrating. Playing football, for instance, was difficult as he wanted to get all of the goals and he would not pass the ball to any of his teammates. Tempers would soon flare and at that point language would fail Rashid. In times of great anxiety he could only rely on his body language to get the message across; the result would be many fights and few friends.

Perhaps the one thing that helped Rashid's social credibility was the fact that computer technology seemed to come as naturally to him as breathing. It was amazing to adults and peers alike to watch Rashid at work.

Within his school day Rashid would need a period of separation from the hectic activities, which would continue one after another. As lessons progressed, one could see the physical changes experienced by him. Due to the demands of the lessons, the social settings for every lesson, the change of subject matter and his high levels of anxiety, Rashid would become very hot. He would perspire and this feeling would only add to his discomfort. Without a time away from everyone Rashid would become very agitated. He would physically become challenging.

Hopefully, these two case studies give a flavour of the types of strengths which children with ASD may have and also illustrate the areas that lead to many challenges, both for the pupils themselves and for the parents and professionals involved. Both pupils have a diagnosis of ASD. Both pupils are individuals, with their own learning styles, and both must be seen initially as children in their own right. Yet the common elements in both case studies can be seen in the broad categories of

1. Communication/language
2. Social abilities
3. Rigidity of thought and imagination

In addition to this there needs to be a consideration of the elements of sensory sensitivity, which must be viewed on an individual basis. A more in-depth discussion of this will follow later in the chapter.

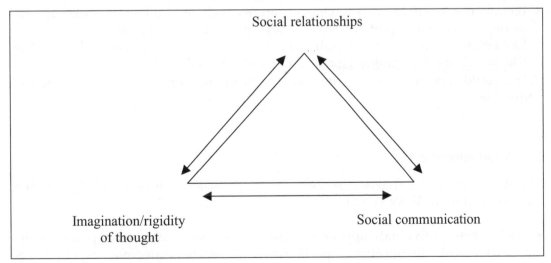

Figure 2.1 The Triad of Impairments

The Triad – a description

As can be seen from Figure 2.1, all three areas of impairment or difference are linked to and have an effect on each other. So how do the differences in the three areas manifest themselves to the observer?

1. Social communication

There is a lack of understanding of communication – the fact that there must be a 'listener' to communicate with and to. Also a lack of recognition of the needs of the listener is evident in their interactions if they are using spoken language. This lack of understanding and inability to communicate manifests itself in the following ways:

- Difficulty in using and making sense of non-verbal and verbal communication – being unable to understand and interpret the facial expressions of others and equally producing inappropriate facial expressions themselves, e.g. smiling when someone is angry, and being unable to process spoken language effectively.
- 'Scripted' speech – being able to recite the entire script of 'The Jungle Book' using all the correct voices for the different characters and a strong American accent. One boy known to the authors always asked the same questions of everyone he met – 'What kind of car do you drive? What colour is it? Does it use petrol or diesel?' On the initial meeting these questions would seem acceptable enough and the boy would apparently absorb all the answers. It was only on subsequent meetings that it would become obvious that he asked everyone the same three questions every time he met them!
- Echolalia (repetition of words and/or phrases either immediately after they have been spoken by another person or delayed until later) – this is a part of normal development that children go through but people with ASD often become 'stuck' in this stage.
- Repetitive questioning – this may be because they have not processed and understood the answer or it may be because they enjoy the sound of the words.
- Lack of or inappropriate intonation – individuals may have no apparent intonation in their voices or use it in such a way that makes their speech sound slightly odd.
- Inability to maintain two-way conversations – they may not respond to a question, not realising that an answer is required, or they may interrupt as they cannot understand the 'give and take' of conversation.
- Literal interpretation of language – phrases such as 'Pull your socks up' can cause an outburst particularly if they are not wearing any or they may immediately bend over and pull them up. One child when asked the question 'Do you know the capital city of America?' by the head teacher replied 'Yes'. He could not understand the hidden meaning behind the head teacher's question.

2. Social interaction

The impairment or difference in their social interaction can be divided into three types according to Wing (1996):

- *aloof*, where individuals appear to ignore or avoid contact with people – this can be most disconcerting, particularly as teachers do not expect to be ignored!
- *passive*, where individuals do not initiate contact with other people but are quite willing to respond when approached by someone – this can become frustrating for the person working with the individual as they have the responsibility for maintaining the interaction
- *active but odd*, where individuals try to interact with other people but not in appropriate ways, such as giving total strangers cuddles or asking repetitive questions but paying little attention to the answers.

Other differences in their social interactions can be shown in the following ways:

- Use of eye contact – they may not look at you when our social rules say that they should make eye contact, or may use their peripheral vision to look at you. Some individuals with ASD look at people too intensely and make one feel distinctly uncomfortable!
- Lack of awareness of personal space – they may quite happily sit on your lap when they want to but become upset when you sit too close to them (in their opinion).
- No/little awareness of the give and take of conversation and the social 'signals' which indicate when it is their turn to communicate.
- Inability to 'read' facial expressions and body language.
- Inappropriate social behaviour – always wanting to be at the front of the queue.
- Apparent lack of empathy – understanding that a kick will hurt them but unable to understand that when they kick someone else that person experiences pain as well.

3. Rigidity of thought and imagination

These differences may be shown in the following ways:

- Difficulty in flexible thought, which may lead to resistance to change in routines, surroundings or people working with them.
- Obsessive or ritualistic behaviour such as lining up cars instead of playing with them, only being interested in trains, rocking or flapping their hands.
- Lack of imaginative or meaningful play (although what they do has a meaning for them which is not easily recognisable by the observer).
- Difficulties with learning incidentally – just because it happened once does not mean that they will know how to act/behave the next time it happens.
- Difficulties in making connections between experiences, which makes generalising knowledge difficult – being able to count up to five counters accurately in the classroom with a particular classroom assistant does not mean that they are able to count up to five apples on a tree in their back garden with their parent.
- Sometimes difficulties with self-organisation – not being able to pack their school bag with the necessary books for the day even though they may be able to say which lessons they have that day.
- Difficulty with creative work – an inability to think creatively in play and work as they may lack a sense of themselves and an imagination.
- Little understanding of danger – our ability to imagine a car knocking us down and the subsequent consequences makes us understand the danger of stepping off the pavement without first checking that the road is clear. Individuals with ASD are unable to imagine the consequences of their actions and therefore have little concept of danger.

From autism to autistic spectrum disorders via Asperger's syndrome

'Autism' was around long before all manner of professionals cropped up to study it, work with it or claim to be able to treat or cure it. (Williams 1996, p. 7)

Uta Frith (1989) describes two documented cases of individuals from the late eighteenth and early nineteenth centuries. The 'wild boy of Aveyron' and Kaspar Hauser appeared to exhibit the behaviours we now associate with and understand as autism. Autism or autistic spectrum disorders (ASD), as it is now termed, was first used as a diagnosis as recently as 1943 by Leo Kanner, a psychiatrist working in Baltimore in America. It was Kanner who first used the term 'early infantile autism' to describe a group of patients he was treating. From that point onwards the condition became a clinical entity and could be recognised and diagnosed. Nowadays we realise that ASD is a lifelong disorder and not just confined to childhood.

Hans Asperger, working in Vienna in 1944 and unaware of Kanner's work, described a group of children who displayed similar behaviours to Kanner's group. A comparison of Kanner's autism and Asperger's syndrome are featured in Figure 2.2. Asperger published his papers in German towards the end of the war and it took some time for them to appear in English literature. It is only in the last ten to fifteen years or so that the term Asperger's syndrome has been used as a diagnosis. It is usually used to describe individuals who have similar impairments to individuals with ASD but who tend to exhibit higher linguistic and intellectual abilities. The debate as to whether Asperger's syndrome is part of the autistic spectrum or an entirely separate condition is still unresolved in some quarters.

Kanner's autism	Asperger's syndrome
☐ Inability to relate affectively to people and situations from early years	☐ Lack of reciprocity and empathy in social interactions although a degree of interaction is desired
☐ An anxiously obsessive desire for the maintenance of sameness	☐ A reliance on repetitive routines and a need for sameness in environments
☐ Ability to memorise things by rote	☐ An ability to memorise details within a narrow field of interest
☐ Lack of spoken language or use of language without communicative intent	☐ Formal speech developed early but delivery tends to be mechanical and content can be odd and pedantic
☐ Over-sensitivity to external and internal stimuli	☐ Over-sensitivity to external and internal stimuli
☐ A fascination for objects such as leaves, lids or string, which are handled with skill and dexterity	☐ Motor clumsiness – gait and posture can be different

Figure 2.2 A comparison of Kanner's autism and Asperger's syndrome

In the 1970s Lorna Wing and Judith Gould studied all children under the age of 15 in the former London Borough of Camberwell to ascertain a clearer definition of autism and to see how it related to other conditions in childhood, including learning difficulties and language impairments. Their findings led to the definition of autistic spectrum disorders in terms of the Triad of Impairment. Wing (1996) states that, although at the time Asperger's syndrome was not known to them, they have since concluded that Kanner's classic autism and Asperger's syndrome were sub-groups amongst a range of disorders, which affected social interaction and communication. Their other conclusions were that the disorders could be associated with any level of intelligence and that other physical conditions and developmental disorders could also be associated with autistic spectrum disorders but not necessarily. Autistic spectrum disorders is the term used to describe a wide range of disorders of development described by the Triad of Impairment.

The search for causes

It is a scientific version of the House that Jack Built. (Wing 1996, p. 78)

Lorna Wing discusses the major ways that researchers are investigating causation. She identified three strands to this work:

- Original causes – a variety of other difficulties such as complications at the pre-natal stage, genetic factors and family histories are all being studied.
- The pathology of the brain – studies are investigating how the brain functions and also the neurochemicals, which are involved in the transmission of messages. The developments of new technologies are assisting with this research.
- Psychological dysfunctions – the latest research is referred to as Theory of Mind (Baron-Cohen 1996), i.e. how the person with ASD understands the thoughts and feelings of others.

What becomes obvious is the fact that there is no one cause of ASD. Case histories reflect this fact and so investigations may be more beneficial in identifying sets of triggers, which combine to make a pathway, resulting in ASD.

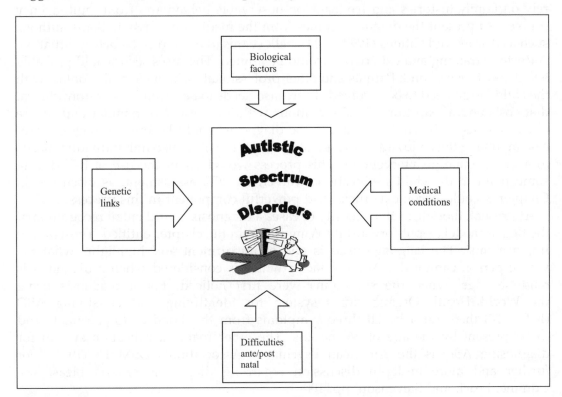

Figure 2.3 Associated triggers linked with autistic spectrum disorders

Autistic spectrum disorders and other features

Wing and Gould's study highlighted the fact that ASD can and does occur with other conditions and features apart from the core Triad of Impairments. These can include:

- poor motor coordination including clumsiness, odd gait and posture;
- over- or under-activity;
- difficulties with language, which include literal understanding, difficulty with comprehension and use of speech as in developmental language disorders;
- different responses to sensory stimuli (these will be discussed later in this chapter);

- changes in mood such as excitement or misery sometimes for no obvious reason (to us);
- unusual eating, drinking or sleeping patterns, which do not coincide with most people's routines;
- neurological and physical disabilities such as epilepsy, Tourette's syndrome, sensory impairments, Down's syndrome or dyspraxia;
- developmental disorders which affect language, reading, writing and number work;
- 'difficult' behaviours such as aggression, self-injury, running away, screaming, spitting and biting;
- psychiatric conditions such as depression, anxiety, obsessive-compulsive disorder, catatonia and 'psychotic states'.

The diagnostic route

There is no easy route towards a diagnosis of ASD. For all concerned, the ride to a formal acknowledgement of the nature of the difficulties can be a long and arduous one. There is no single medical test that can offer a definitive diagnosis. Professionals rely on family histories and feedback on observable behaviours from multi-agency sources. At present the diagnosis comes from the medical profession. Some authors, such as Aarons and Gittens (1992, p. 11), believe this to be an unsatisfactory situation. A doctor's training and experience would be limited. The cases seen would probably be the most severe kind. Parents and other professionals who have daily contact with the child/adult need to be involved. There also needs to be a trend away from clinical diagnosis and a leap towards observations within a variety of familiar and secure environments. This would mean that the diagnosis would become an ongoing process involving the child/adult to a greater extent. It would also link individual needs to a programme of intervention. This process would entail the use of ICT during some point in the child's educational career. An ICT assessment, as discussed in Chapter 5, could become a crucial and powerful component in this process.

At present, though, in the majority of cases a diagnosis would entail recognition of the deficit model as put forward by Wing (1996) in the chapter entitled 'The Triad of Impairments'. The language used is one of impairment and highlights what the young person cannot do. Another factor which is considered when a diagnosis is made is 'age' when the symptoms were first noticed. For a diagnosis using the World Health Organization's system for identifying and classifying ASD (ICD – 10) there must be all three symptoms from the Triad of Impairments and to be present by the age of 36 months. The other main classification system for diagnosing ASD is the American Psychiatric Association's DSM IV (1994). For further and more in-depth discussion regarding diagnostic criteria please see Cumine, Leach and Stevenson, pp. 100–1.

The authors would like to suggest that an alternative title be used. It should read as the 'Triad of Differences'. This would mean that all people involved would be aware of the fact that this group of children *can* communicate (and very effectively at times), they *can* operate within a social situation (albeit in a limited and unusual way), and their rigidity of behaviour and thought *can* be the result of sensory and other stress factors. This is an oversimplification but one which is grounded on a *'can do'* model.

Sensory sensitivity

The Triad of Impairments/Differences does not entirely cover difficulties experienced by individuals. The additional dimension that needs to be addressed is that of sensory sensitivity. Through taking note of autobiographical accounts of how the senses are processed by people with ASD, it becomes clear that individuals may be hyper- or hypo-sensitive to sounds, light, touch, smell and taste. Any single sense or combination of senses may override other perceptions and cause distractions, resulting in distorted vision or hearing for instance. These unusual sensory responses are again unique to each individual. The pupil in the introductory chapter could name the computer make through listening to the humming noise it emitted; other pupils might recoil from environments with bright strip lights, as these would prove too painful. Both Temple Grandin (1995) and Donna Williams (1998) describe their own sensory sensitivities. In *Thinking in Pictures* Grandin states that she was a child who was a pressure seeker, someone who would need to wrap themselves in blankets to initiate the whole bodily sense of pressure. However, this was only a positive experience when she initiated it and not when it was with another person.

> *Being touched triggered flight; it flipped my circuit breaker.* (p. 62)

As an alternative to human touch, she invented her 'squeeze machine', which she had the power to adjust appropriately, controlling it completely. This ability to control and hold 'power to adjust' is very much an attribute of ICT, which we explore in more detail in Chapter 4 (the 'automatic' and 'provisional' qualities of ICT). In addition, Williams (1996) reflects upon 'emotional hypersensitivity', stating that there are many different aspects to this but the one she explores is mostly related to the 'self–other' sensitivity of becoming saturated in trying to find meanings in relation to another's body messages, or over-exposure to emotions. Perhaps Figure 2.4 illustrates what might be a fuller picture of a pupil with ASD.

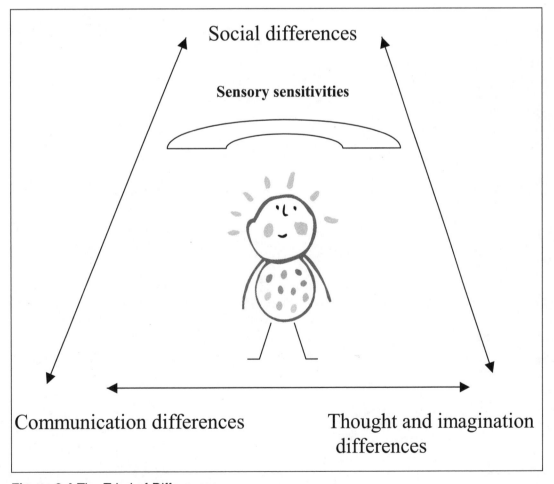

Figure 2.4 The Triad of Differences

If one's sensory perceptions are disconnected, disjointed or in some way distorted, then a person could experience high anxiety levels and exhibit behaviour that would be perceived by observers as irrational. This is an enormously important area to think about when working with pupils. However it is doubly so when using computer technology with an individual who has ASD. In Chapter 4 we suggest that ICT has immense potential to allow both carers and children to control and moderate the environment in which they learn. Programs can be loud, bright, fast and intrusive for some pupils. Careful observation of students' reactions to participation in computer interactions is essential. It may mean adapting programs, using headphones or running them without sound at all. An individual's preferences must influence the way we use computers with young people with ASD.

Flo Longhorn (2000, p. 37) brings together the areas of sensory differences and accessing computers by stating that it is the senses that 'breach the barrier into the world of special people and form a platform from which to go forward together in their education . . . A toolbox of skills needs to be offered to the very special learner so he/she can access learning more easily.' For some the 'toolbox of skills' could be in the form of ICT.

3 Beyond the Triad

How children with ASD present in class

The Triad of Differences goes a long way to highlight the difficulties that pupils may experience. However, it does not explain everything. We need to remember and focus on the individual. Amongst the interweave of all of these elements the essence of the pupil must be sought. If, as carers or professionals, we concentrate on the Triad alone then we will gain a very narrow, limited view of the pupil. If, however, we push these boundaries outward, adding to the strengths and expanding the skills for every individual, we will begin to see the person's potential. In this chapter we will try to explain how children with ASD present in social settings, i.e. the class, and how ICT may be used to address areas of differences. We must also reiterate that there are many strategies that are successful in aiding the student's progression, and ICT is only one of them. We must always be aware of the individual's needs. To do this effectively we will look beyond the Triad, becoming detectives and investigating the differences.

Figure 3.1 Becoming a detective

Some early reactions to ASD

Encountering children with ASD for the first time can be baffling, frustrating and confusing. They somehow challenge your conditioned responses to situations and throw your expectations upside down. Here are some quotes from professionals who later came to understand a little more about autism by working with the individual, and not the triad:

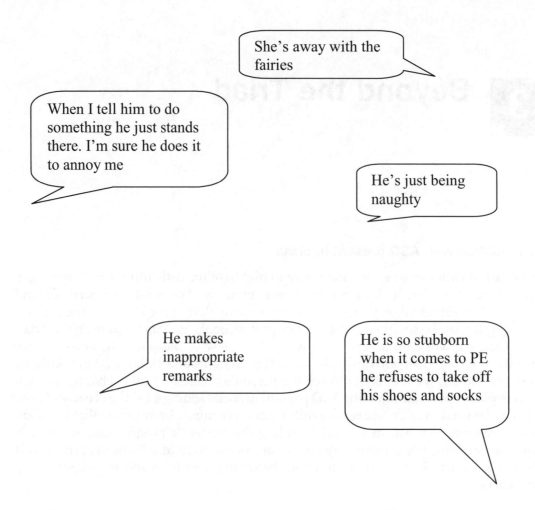

It is about time we exploded these 'myths' in order to bring about a change in the way we teach pupils with ASD.

Figure 3.3 Exploding the myths

What follows is a sequence of three tables that illustrates how school staff may experience pupils with ASD within early years, primary and secondary phases. They are over-generalisations and in no way cover the whole range of pupils, since all are individual. However it is hoped that some part of what is described can be recognised within your work settings. Also, the tables in no way illustrate the efforts by settings to change the environmental factors which, as reflective practitioners, we would do to influence and enhance the learning situations.

Early years phase

Times	Monday	Description of difficulties
8.55 a.m.	Registration	Pupil reluctant to come across threshold, needing physical intervention. *Pupil upset because registration area has been moved.* Pupil comes into class, hangs up coat and sits on carpet in the corner.
9 a.m.	Inside play	Pupil tries to leave the class to gain access to the garden. When this is not allowed he then begins to bang his head with his fist. *When calmer, the pupil will seek out his favourite object and 'play' in a very rigid manner.* Pupil will sit at the activity, in the presence of an adult, and interact verbally with the adult alone, perhaps getting possessive over adult and resources.
9.30 a.m.	Free play outside and inside	When access to garden finally allowed, the pupil races for favourite bike or ball and gets distraught if another child has their turn. *Pupil always on the periphery of the garden area, solitary play, ignoring peer interaction.* Pupil always seeming to get into squabbles with peers, as he wants to dominate play equipment and has difficulty taking turns. Difficulty initiating play with peers.
11 a.m.	Group story time	Pupil is reluctant to join the group on the carpet area, he has only a few words, which he uses inappropriately, and he find focusing on a book difficult. *Pupil joins group for a short time, using a carpet square as a reminder of behaviour, but shared focus and book is meaningless.* When pupil realises it is story time he strides across peers to get to the front and wants the story to go at his pace, with him alone opening flaps, answering questions.
11.30 a.m.	Home time	Parent/carer is asked to come a little earlier to pick up pupil as he finds the transition time difficult to handle, the unstructured wait is frustrating for him. *Parent/carer is not noticed by pupil, who is occupying himself with shiny sequins dropped on the floor during the session and he becomes upset when he has to leave.* Pupil enjoys routine of calling peers' names out as their parent/carers come; showing fantastic memory but also has to be the last one to leave because of this.

Primary phase

Times	Monday	Description of difficulties
9 a.m.	Registration	Pupil enters classroom supported by LSA, sits in usual place on carpet with LSA close by. Becomes restless after name has been called for register and starts to make noises. LSA takes pupil to work station for activities. *Pupil enters classroom and sits on the carpet close to the teacher. Interrupts registration as wants to tell teacher about his trains.*
9.15 a.m.	Literacy hour	Pupil sits on carpet in special place with LSA close by. Teacher reads Big Book. Pupil's attention is focused by LSA as does not look towards teacher. Pupil starts to fiddle with shoes, licking finger and wiping over sole of shoe. Leans towards child nearest and wipes wet finger on their shoe. Begins to rock and make noise and is taken to table by LSA to do differentiated activity linked to literacy hour. *Pupil sits close to the teacher. Looks at Big Book but continually interrupts as wants to comment on the pictures. Stands up to see a particular picture and has to be reminded that other pupils cannot see the book. Apparently listens to instructions about the activity but when the class disperses pupil remains seated on carpet unsure of what to do. Teacher re-explains the task, pupil goes to seat and manages to write name. At end of lesson pupil has looked around classroom, watched the other pupils, interfered with their work and completed very little work.*
10.15 a.m.	Assembly	Pupil goes into assembly at the end of the class line accompanied by LSA. Pupil sits at the end of the class line, fiddles with shoe and then lies down. When song is sung pupil covers ears and starts to scream. Pupil taken back to classroom to calm down. *Pupil sits with class in the hall. Teacher taking assembly asks questions of the whole school about the story being read to them. Pupil raises hand but shouts out answers without being chosen. Reminded to wait until asked. Pupil surprises staff by knowing the answer to a question that no other pupils are able to answer.*
10.35 a.m.	Playtime	Pupil spends whole of playtime running around the edge of the playground, occasionally stopping to spin on the spot. Ignores attempts at interaction by other pupils. *Pupil plays chasing game with small group of peers. Then loses interest and joins a game of football. Runs up and down with peers but does not actively participate in the game. Group seem unaware of pupil's desire to be included in the game.*

10.55 a.m.	Numeracy hour	Pupil unwilling to come in from the playground. Eventually comes in and joins class. Sits on the carpet, stretches legs out and keeps touching back of pupil in front, distracting them from lesson. Told to stop and starts to kick harder so is taken for a walk by LSA. Returns to lesson and starts to scream because another child is using the computer. Is persuaded to calm down and wait. Works on a simple numeracy program on the computer. Is able to use the mouse and to complete the program. Goes back over favourite parts of the program. *Pupil sits on carpet and joins in loudly with the counting activity that the class is doing. Comments loudly that a peer is not joining in because they cannot do it. Needs activity explained and modelled, then completes it very quickly and accurately. Has an opportunity to work on the computer and announces loudly that the program is too easy even though pupil is unable to complete it properly.*
12 noon	Lunchtime	Has packed lunch as will only eat limited foods – then similar behaviour to morning playtime. *Eats school lunch very slowly – then similar behaviour to morning playtime.*
1 p.m.	Science	Lesson on shadows does not understand concept so taken outside in the sunshine to look at shadow. Does not understand and runs around. Is brought back to classroom and covers whole worksheet with black pencil. *Pupil is fascinated by different shadow shapes and draws lots of shapes on back of worksheet, ignoring the activity on the front.*
2.15 p.m.	PE	Pupil needs help to get changed. Once in hall, runs around making noise. Does not react to teacher's instructions and rolls about on mats in the corner. Class practise ball skills but pupil wants to hold the ball all the time instead of passing it to other pupils. Needs help to get dressed. *Pupil gets changed but puts T-shirt on inside out. In hall joins in warm up activities and ball skill practice. Has difficulty with catching and throwing – accuses another pupil of deliberately throwing the ball too high (which is not true). Group needs teacher intervention to start activity again – pupil continues to complain. After PE dresses very slowly.*

Secondary phase

Times	Monday	Description of difficulties
8.40 a.m.	Registration	Secondary school much larger than previously experienced and pupil finds the environment threatening, confusing and stressful. *Pupil coming into school and class at exactly the same time via the same route but becoming anxious because peers were changing their timings and order into class.*
8.50 a.m.	Modern foreign languages	Pupil uses single words only and not consistently. The French lesson contains no functional meaning, yet he enjoyed last week's 'French tasting' session. *Pupil likes to use set phrases in French but soon becomes irritated by certain pupils making mistakes. He will then get very load and challenging.*
9.50 a.m.	Geography	The geography of the school building is a constant source of threat to the pupil. He needs an adult to facilitate his movement throughout the building. *The pupil's ability to memorise factual knowledge has given him certain kudos within this subject area, however generalising this knowledge is difficult.*
10.50 a.m.	Break	Pupil spends majority of break time swinging round and round the basketball hoop in the playground. There is no peer interaction and an assistant is with him constantly. *Fight ensues during a game of football when pupil insists on being captain, goalie and striker all in one.*
11.10 a.m.	Literacy hour	Picture Exchange Communication System is being introduced and pupil works in a 1 : 1 situation to practise these exchanges. *Pupil refuses to join in any group work and remains in his seat reading his favourite book 'This is literacy'.*
12.10 a.m.	Religious education	By now the pupil is becoming restless. His internal clock is telling him that it is lunchtime and he can now smell food cooking. Difficulty in focusing him on classroom tasks and pupil is becoming disruptive. *Traditional chalk and talk lesson and pupil enjoys working on his own.*
1.10 p.m.	Lunch	At last! Pupil rushes to dining hall and proceeds to run to the front of the line. Lunchtime supervisor insists he goes to the end of the line. Major tantrum erupts. *Luckily today there is the pupil's favourite choice. Yet someone is sitting in his favourite place and he cannot eat at any other table. A staff member intervenes and explains things to the seated pupil who willingly moves.*
2.20 p.m.	Art	Still very upset over lunchtime episode. Gets to lesson late with Learning Assistant but manages to join in the practical part of lesson and enjoys it. *Pupil shows aptitude in this area and works alone to complete course work.*

Implications for teaching and learning

Hopefully you will now be able to identify with some of the pupil's difficulties. Even if you have not been in the presence of a young person with a diagnosis of ASD you may have an inkling, or an intuitive reaction, when reading through the descriptions of the variety of behaviours which may occur throughout a school day. It is important to remember that, to be effective in addressing the pupil's needs, you must liaise with everyone who has contact with him or her. That includes family members and other professionals. Of course this is 'good practice', and systems that support this will indeed aid all pupils.

For the next part of the chapter we would like to address the implications for teaching and learning and make links with the relevance and use of ICT with students with ASD. The following chapters will focus more closely on many of the issues, but an overview will first be presented. The strategies discussed are not a finite list but should be viewed as pointers. The other factor which needs to be constantly to the fore is the personality of the pupil, as this will help prioritise the next steps and plan for future work; remember the 'can do' model. See the pupil's strengths positively and plan progress by using ICT.

Ways forward in the three areas of the Triad of Impairments or Differences

Area of difference	Range of strategies
Social interaction	• Get to know the person with autism: what is important to them; how they interact; notice what they are looking at or doing • Use their interests to get their attention and to extend your intervention • Work on one area at a time – try to ensure positive social interaction and communication • Set achievable targets, recognising the limitations of the individual. Too high expectations can cause failure, frustration and anger • Encourage eye contact on initial interaction, i.e. saying their name. Some individuals with autism receive information better from peripheral rather than central gaze vision – allow them to use 'their way of looking' • It may be necessary to set up 'friendship groups', or a 'buddy' system, to decrease reliance on an adult. These may be a basis for a social skills group or 'circle of friends' group • Use turn taking games and mutual help activities • Be consistent
Relevance of ICT	• Pupil's interest in visual and auditory information is enhanced by computer generated images • Working at a computer is non-threatening and does not involve understanding social cues • Computers provide a positive basis for the beginnings of social interactions such as turn taking, sharing and developing awareness of 'another' • Computers are consistent, predictable and controllable • Levels of programs can be decided upon to ensure pupil success • Computers can present single focus activities (see reference to Murray in Chapter 5) • Certain skills such as learning to play chess on the computer by more able pupils with autism can be transferred to the playing chess with another person • Self-esteem can be enhanced by pupil success on the computer • A vast number of pupils with ASD like computers and are motivated by their use

Area of difference	Range of strategies
Social communication	• Gain pupil's attention before trying to communicate with them by using their name • Use minimal, clear language. Be specific • Give pupil time to process language • Use relevant objects to aid understanding • Use of signing or gesture can help some people. These need to be clear. The pupil also needs to understand that in order to communicate with another person using signing or gesture the person needs to be looking at them • Visual cues can be used to support verbal language • Metaphors and colloquial speech will confuse the pupil • Shouting at pupils could cause pain if they are hypersensitive to sound and will only cause them to become distressed • Sometimes pupils with autism may appear to be deaf or hearing impaired as they may not automatically respond to their name, but this is frequently because they do not have an understanding of the concept of communication
Relevance of ICT	• Using headphones (if the pupil will tolerate them), adjusted to the correct volume for the individual, can help to focus the pupil on the computer activity and decrease distractibility • Explore programs which encourage vocalisations from the pupil • Computers use visual images, which are highly motivating for a pupil. Therefore they may be tempted to share the use of the computer and communicate with another person in order to have their turn, which may not be the case when participating in a different activity • Adjusting the settings of the hardware and software allows pupil time to process any sounds or language generated by the computer • Sections of particular programs can be easily repeated including the sounds, e.g. talking books • Some pupils with autism will respond verbally to the computer as any language used is always the same and they do not need to make sense of any social cues • Programs such as 'Clicker', 'Writing with Symbols' and 'Inclusive Writer' are useful to aid communication from adult to child, or child to adult. They can also be used to aid the child's understanding of the written word by providing symbols to trigger memory • Several augmentative and alternative communication devices (AAC) are worth trying

Area of difference	Range of strategies
Imagination/ rigidity of thought	• Never assume that the pupil with autism knows what you intend to do next • Make the plan of the day clear – give structure, obvious beginnings and endings • Teach pupils with autism how to play – in the classroom and in the playground • Teach about emotions – verbalise – make pupils aware of how they are feeling during an activity • Teach new skills through modelling, parallel work or direct teaching – draw pupil's attention to salient features of the lesson • Build in time every lesson to reflect on what the pupil has experienced and learnt and how that relates to past learning and future experiences • Teach the same activity in different situations and with different people • Move on from adult cueing to self-cueing, i.e. pupil commenting on his/her actions at the time, or use photographs or videos to help the pupil reflect on the activity
Relevance of ICT	• Computers are predictable which makes them a positive experience for pupils with autism • Programs have clear beginnings and endings • Choices and options are clearly presented • Computer games programs can develop the idea of interaction – initially between the child and the computer but gradually extending this play to include another pupil • Word processing can make work appear perfect – any mistakes can be easily rectified. Some pupils with autism can become frustrated and upset if they make a mistake in their handwritten work. • There are programs that address emotional issues such as facial expressions and help the pupil to become more aware of their own and others' emotions. Brilliant Computing produces 'Smart Alex' where the pupil can change simple facial expressions. (Granada Learning) • Visual cues can be quickly produced with the use of a digital camera and computer so that the pupil has an almost instant reminder of a recently completed activity • Programs such as 'Clicker' grids can present images and words on screen to act as a 'writing frame', as a reminder of content and sequence

Finally what follows is an example of a profile that can be used by professionals and parents/carers to record the strengths and abilities of a child. It may also be useful in showing how progress is made and pointers to what needs to be focused on next. However the progression will not necessarily be linear and the profile is not an exhaustive one. For a more comprehensive 'Observation Profile' we would guide the readers to Val Cumine, Julia Leach and Gill Stevenson's (2000, pp. 93–99) extensive work.

The profile would also be different for pupils with Asperger's syndrome. In such cases, more emphasis would be on working with computers to encourage self-confidence and focus on developing positive social contact (see Chapter 4). It becomes even more important to 'know' the child or young adult, the way they react to and perceive others, their use of language, any sensory sensitivities, etc. A person-centred collation of observations and targets would enhance the individualised profile.

Tony Attwood (1998) adds another dimension to the use of ICT and Asperger's syndrome. He states that specific interest in using computers should be encouraged as it '. . . may also be a source of relaxation and enjoyment . . . Indulgence in the interest is almost therapeutic.' (p. 99) This issue must be addressed by those professionals who believe that allowing a pupil access to a computer should be in a reward situation only. ICT needs to be an integral learning tool, a bridge to positive social contact and a means of relaxation, a calming device.

Drawing together information on autism and moving on to look at ICT

The following pupil profile should help you draw together the information in Chapters 2 and 3 and focus it on a specific pupil. Similarly we have tried to summarise the qualities of ICT in a diagrammatic way at the end of Chapter 4, with the 'star' diagram. We hope that used together these diagrams should begin to help you match a particular pupil to likely ICT solutions. We offer some practical examples of this approach within the case studies in Chapter 5.

Pupil profile

Pupil name:	D.O.B.		Class:	

Social interaction	Not present	Emerging date	Mastered date
Interested in visual information			
Interested in auditory information			
Shows interest in computer			
Attempts to touch computer hardware			
Leads adult to computer			
Touches screen			
Touches mouse			
Masters mouse			
Touches keyboard			
Tolerates adult guidance			
Recognises photo of computer			
Recognises symbol of computer			
Tolerates limitations of time and program directed by adult			
Tolerates peers alongside whilst at computer			
Takes turns at computer with adult			
Takes turns at computer with peer			
Acknowledges adult directives			
Acknowledges peer directives			
Negotiates with peer re: program			
Social communication			
Uses photo or symbol to indicate wish for computer			
Uses vocalisation/words to indicate wish for computer			
Specifically requests a certain program			
Responds positively to voice activated programs			
Tolerates headphones			
Able to work with Clicker program			
Imitates sounds/words from program appropriately			
Generalises one or two words during other relevant activities			
Will adjust sound or program levels to control computer			
Rigidity of thought			
Knows routine turning on computer; can do independently			
Completes program 1–2 times during a computer session			
Will react positively to new software, one change at a time			

©2002 Colin Hardy, Jan Ogden, Julie Newman and Sally Cooper. *Autism and ICT*. Published by David Fulton Publishers. ISBN 1-85436-824-X.

4 The special qualities of ICT – a rationale

In the opening chapter of this book we quoted a range of sources – parents, teachers support workers and children with ASD – all of whom were fervent in their enthusiasm for ICT. Underlying this faith in ICT, whether consciously acknowledged or not, are assumptions about the fashion in which children learn and the attributes of ICT. Chapters 2 and 3 examined in more detail the way in which children with ASD learn and some of the more commonly encountered problems in the classroom and home. Some ICT applications have already been suggested. The purpose of this chapter is to define more clearly the special qualities of ICT and how they may be employed to the best advantage for a range of pupils with ASD and associated language and communication difficulties.

What is ICT?

Information Technology (IT) is a term used to cover a whole range of hardware and software associated with computers. The word 'Communication' was added recently to form the term Information and Communication Technology (ICT). This reflects the increasing use of networks and in particular the Internet and the added potential that this provides for communication.

The definition of what is covered by the term ICT is offered by the Qualification and Curriculum Authority (QCA/DfEE 1999, p. 184) within the review of the National Curriculum for England:

> In the context of the school curriculum, the term information and communication technology (ICT) is used to refer to the range of tools and techniques relating to computer-based hardware and software; to communications including both directed and broadcast; to information sources such as CD-ROM and the Internet, and to associated technologies such as robots, video conferencing and digital TV.

In other words ICT is a broad term that covers much more than just computers and includes augmentative and alternative communication (AAC), video, radio, television and so on.

Will ICT aid a pupil with ASD?

The special qualities of ICT are often alluded to in general terms or assumed without question; for example, the interactive nature of ICT is frequently mentioned almost as a 'cure all' for any pupil with special educational needs. It is clearly important for teachers, support staff and others to have a means to investigate the potential of ICT in a more detailed and systematic way. Two important questions arise:

- firstly, in the words of the Teacher Training Agency (1998) there is the need 'to know when the use of ICT is beneficial to achieve teaching objectives in the subject and phase, and when the use of ICT would be less effective or inappropriate';

- secondly, if ICT is felt to be beneficial there is then the need for a more detailed analysis of which ICT applications are most likely to aid an individual pupil with ASD.

In a former book, *ICT for All*, Colin Hardy (2000) proposed five qualities of ICT that are relevant to pupils said to have 'special educational needs'. These will be used here as a starting point but with particular emphasis on how these qualities relate to children with ASD.

A qualities model for ICT

The approach adopted here could be called a 'qualities model' as it attempts to draw out 'generic qualities' of ICT. These are later presented in a spider diagram framework that should assist class teachers and others when initially trying to identify which software and hardware may help any pupil with ASD.

These 'generic qualities' of ICT are based on the Teacher Training Agency ICT curriculum for teaching staff (1998), experience of working with children, a review of current research and literature on ICT and autism, and discussions with staff, parents and children. Readers may agree or disagree with the number and types of qualities but what is important is to move beyond the popular belief that ICT is good for pupils with autism, to a clearer definition of exactly what are the qualities that we aim to appropriate for the purposes of increasing curriculum access for a specific pupil:

1. The automatic features of ICT

Figure 4.1 See the wood from the trees

The automatic features of ICT (automaticity) enable pupils to perform mundane and dull operations quickly and easily and so focus their attention on the main purposes of the learning.

Databases and spreadsheets are often associated with the quality of automaticity as they allow large amounts of data to be quickly and simply analysed and trends and patterns more easily picked out. In addition such programs often have the facility to automatically produce reports with beautiful graphs and diagrams, which can be a bonus for children whose handwriting and drawing may be poor (Grandin 2000a).

This must be a quality worth exploiting for those pupils with ASD who are said to:

- be easily distracted;
- have poor organisational skills;
- be obsessed by detail, failing to see a general rule or overall pattern or picture.

Mike Blamires (1999) suggests some database programs worth investigation:

> *Two simple programs for this are Counter (Blackcat) in which a set of numerical data can be displayed using a variety of graphs and Clipboard (Blackcat) which is a simple database that is also quite powerful. This comes with sets of information that directly address national curriculum topics Living World (birds, mini beasts, food), Changes (explorers, materials, seasons) and Celebrations (new beginnings, colour, seasons) and Earth In Space. Improved Windows versions are available that also include 'Counting with Pictures', which produces very simple graphs by clicking on icons.*
>
> *Starting Grid (RM) is an introductory spreadsheet which is a subset of the powerful windows program Excel. As well as having options for organising and manipulating information, it can be used for the production of a wide range of charts.*

A readily available example of this type of program, which readers may like to try, is the spreadsheet Excel. This is supplied on a wide range of computers as part of the Microsoft Office suite of programs. With a little help pupils can be shown how to enter a simple set of data, for example favourite types of food. The 'Graph Wizard' will then bring squeals of delight as pupils quickly and easily produce a range of colourful graphs including pie, bar and spider diagrams.

2. Capacity and range

Figure 4.2 Bring the world to the child

The capacity and range of ICT is to store, retrieve and manipulate information from a vast quantity and range of reference and other material.

The two facilities most commonly associated with these qualities are the CD-ROM and the Internet. These offer the potential for what Kaye (1991) calls 'A universal library of all knowledge' which is at a pupil's fingertips.

This can be an important point for children with ASD who to a greater or lesser extent find it hard to cope with the changeable and multiple demands on their attention from the normal environment. Murray (1997) suggests that as a result their attention is tunnelled, interest trapped, its objects isolated and without context. One can sympathise with Rashid in Chapter 2 who 'would need a period of separation from the hectic activities, which would continue one after another'.

The CD and the Internet can bring the world to the child and do so within clear boundaries.

- How much or how little information assails the senses is at the control of the user and events occur in a fixed and predictable order.
- Volume, brightness and shade of colour, speed and quantity of presentation of information are all controllable, as is the means of input, be it through a range of keyboards, touch screen, mouse, tracker ball, joystick, switches concept keyboard. In Murray's words (1997), 'restricted stimuli in all sensory modalities'.
- There is no need to access or integrate information from the external environment. Again quoting from Murray, computers are a 'contained event receptacle'.

There is a danger that a person already isolated from the world will retreat even more 'into the computer'. But Murray (1997) and others reject this.

- The computer is a bridge into the real world which starts where the child is.
- The therapeutic qualities of the computer make it a more pleasant arena in which to encounter, albeit secondhand, the real world.
- Computing in the home or school is seldom an isolated activity, frequently attracting the attention and interest of others and frequently requiring resource to others for help or to share interest. It is a stimulus to social and communication opportunities.

3. The provisional qualities of ICT

Figure 4.3 Be forgiving of mistakes

Provisionality is the quality of ICT which allows for ease of correction so that items can be edited, changed and re-arranged with minimum effort.

This is most commonly associated with the improvements in accuracy and appearance of work using word processing (WP) and desktop publishing (DTP). Students feel free to experiment in a forgiving medium where mistakes need not be punished. Underwood and Underwood (1990) suggest that pen and paper teaches us to avoid mistakes above all else, whereas the WP reduces the cost of mistakes and encourages concentration on content. The quick and easy ability to produce professional and neat looking documents gives us the potential to meet the demands for perfection, associated to a greater or lesser extent with a range of pupils who have ASD.

There is a danger of obsession with detail. The language and praise of teachers and carers needs to be on regularity and consistency of word-processed work, rather than glowing praise for individual 'masterpieces'.

4. Interactivity

Figure 4.4 Let your imagination run wild

Interactivity refers to the qualities of ICT, and more particularly multi-media facilities, that allow children to be more actively involved with their learning. Bruner, Piaget and Vygotsky are among the many researchers who stress the need for the active engagement of the learner. For the child with ASD, the interactive potential of ICT can be used to avoid her/him being a passive recipient of knowledge or passive recipient of communication.

For early computer use there are no better examples of this quality than the switch programs used to develop awareness of the cause and effect relationship in a child. Switches, and early computer use, are described in Chapter 6.

There are many programs and games for older children that claim to be interactive. But simply bombarding the individual with a cacophony of sound and visual effects is little different from the real world that confronts the child with ASD. Teachers and carers would be well advised to try any software first and in particular ensure that the interactivity can be controlled and customised to suit the particular needs of an individual child.

There is increasing interest in programs that exploit virtual reality as a means to bring real world situations such as roads, kitchens and so on to the child. In this way skills can safely be practised. Current research is considering the degree to which these skills can be transferred back into the real world and how best to achieve this.

5. The social attributes of ICT

Figure 4.5 The go-between

The social attributes of computer use are associated with learning through collaboration and the inter-personal and social skills gained from group work. Scrimshaw (1993) contends that computer use is a social practice and it is through cooperative learning that the greatest gains are to be made.

A range of authors have observed that the public nature of the screen makes it a focus for interaction and collaboration and examples abound of group projects particularly in the field of cooperative writing.

Murray (1997), considering ICT use for pupils with autism, suggests that the computer screen can act as a 'third party' upon whom attention can be focused in a non-threatening way, thus allowing the pupil to build up confidence to relate to a fellow pupils or a teacher who is also present.

Jordan (Jordan and Powell 1990) referring to students on the autistic spectrum notes:

> *unlike other children they are unable or unwilling to rely upon socially and verbally mediated learning and so computer presented activities may be particularly helpful.*

Detheridge (1997), in examining the use of ICT to improve communication for students with severe language and communication difficulties, observed additional gains in terms of improvement in social interaction. She noted that this was facilitated more by portable devices than desktop computers because they tended to be employed in discrete settings and there is here a clear message in terms of the classroom management of ICT equipment for gains, in terms of social interaction, to be maximised.

The star qualities of ICT

Five qualities or attributes for ICT have been proposed here as most relevant to the inclusive setting: automaticity, capacity, provisionality, interactivity and sociability. They are not claimed to be the only qualities of ICT but the ones that are most often found associated with ASD. For most students, more than one of these qualities in varying degrees will have contributed to the effectiveness of ICT. A method suggested to record this is the use of 'star' or 'radar' diagrams. It is intended that this 'model' moves towards the goal outlined in the introduction of helping staff to clarify what are the qualities of ICT and the degree to which each of these can contribute to aiding curriculum access within the specific circumstances relating to a particular pupil's needs.

The 'star qualities' of ICT

The five qualities identified here can be represented on a 'star diagram'. This is helpful as it enables us to consider which of the five qualities apply to any particular pupil and so more quickly focus on the software and hardware that is most likely to be of assistance.

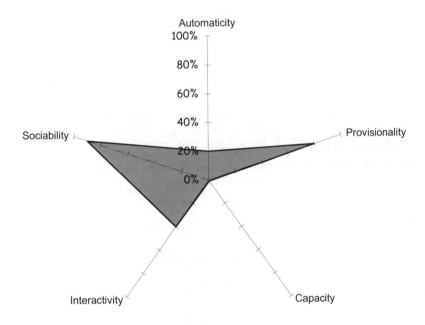

Figure 4.6 The 'star' qualities of ICT

One example of the star diagram (Figure 4.6) has been done here for Trevor, a pupil with ASD.

Trevor's statement described a pupil on the autistic spectrum. At an ICT assessment he took great pleasure in typing in the letters of the alphabet on a talking word processor leaving a space after each to hear their sound. He did similarly with 'My World', dragging and dropping each letter of the alphabet. He seemed to take pleasure in repetition of tasks, dragging and dropping numerous copies of the same dinosaur picture on the same island in another My World screen.

Trevor will not make eye to eye contact with anyone, he will respond to known adults and pupils but seldom initiates any contact. We were therefore surprised that although he had never met me before, he allowed me to sit next to him, responded to some of my questions to him and even volunteered comments about one of the programs that we tried. In all of this conversation the VDU screen acted as a 'third party' with all of the comments and remarks being directed to activities on the screen rather than directly to me.

Entering five values into the spreadsheet 'Excel' produced this and the graph wizard option was used to produce the final diagram. Participants may wish to try this for themselves for a pupil on the autistic spectrum by making use of the blank star diagram (Figure 4.7).

Pupil Name: Age: COP stage:

Pen Picture of a Pupil on the Autistic Spectrum
(Make use of the profile at the end of Chapter 3)

- What qualities of ICT may help this pupil?
- Mark the arms of the spider. Join your points and colour in.

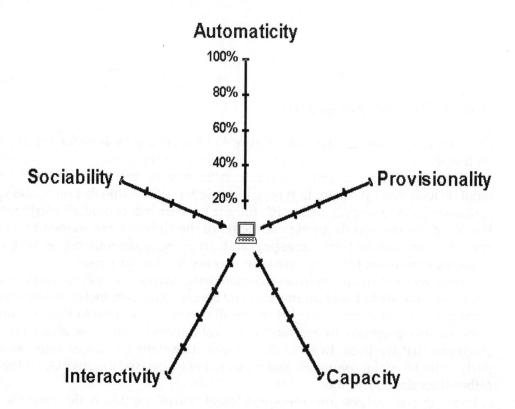

Figure 4.7 Blank star diagram

5 Practical strategies across the autistic spectrum

The preceding chapters have provided information on the nature of ASD and discussed the theoretical relevance of ICT to pupils on the spectrum.

In this chapter we will explore the practical application of various ICT interventions in an educational setting. It will be seen that there are many factors involved in assessing the optimum ICT support for a pupil, and also that success cannot be guaranteed, even in cases where it seems the ideal solution!

Whilst it is evident to many who work in education that ICT provides special opportunities and benefits to these pupils it is not always easy to decide which software and hardware will best assist them. In all the cases discussed here the starting point is the individual pupil and the various aspects of their learning profile. The educational setting and curriculum must, of course, also be taken into account in order for ICT support to have a realistic chance of success.

Successful ICT support

The learning environment

For ICT support to have a long-term impact on pupil achievement the following factors must be considered and incorporated into a support plan:

- The learning style of the pupil. Some pupils with similar levels of apparent need and attainment may require their learning to be mediated in very different ways. It is important to identify how the pupil learns. Some pupils, for example, are visual learners whilst others are auditory learners. One pupil would resist direct instruction but would take an active interest in what others were doing – she was an indirect learner. Others may be 'incidental' learners who absorb fragments of information rather than a coherent structure. This learning style is quite common in pupils with ASD.
- Staff teaching style(s). These should be compatible with the type of support envisaged and it may be necessary to negotiate a different approach to teaching in order to facilitate this.
- The classroom management systems. Again these should enable the introduction of new activities and ways of accessing the curriculum for individual pupils.
- The nature and amount of staff support available to the pupil. It is obviously not going to be useful to expect a support assistant with minimal ICT skills to support a pupil using ICT without the necessary training, which should be considered during the assessment. On the other hand, if support and expertise are available in the classroom, the range of available options increases accordingly.

Curriculum access

ICT support should facilitate inclusion by minimising barriers to curriculum access:

- ICT support should be used alongside other interventions and support as a part of a structured programme of support fitting in with the IEP and other targets and the National Curriculum.
- ICT support should facilitate and support access to the whole curriculum and whole class activities as far as possible.
- Targets should be set for ICT support with clear criteria for success. These should be evaluated, preferably in conjunction with other educational targets at review.

Practical considerations

It is vital for the logistical and practical issues to be considered. In many of the cases in which ICT support fails to be effective this is a major causative factor. The following issues should be addressed during the process of planning the support:

- Location of power points.
- Seating arrangements in class and at the computer should be in accordance with health and safety regulations.
- Arrangements for printing work.
- For secondary aged pupils, movement around the school needs to be considered. Will the support be available in the lessons where it is needed and, if not, how can this be achieved?
- If the ICT support is to be extended to the home, liaison arrangements will need to be put in place to ensure consistency in the use of software such as spelling and literacy programs.
- Keyboard skills – do these need to be developed as part of the support? Should this be undertaken before the support is introduced or alongside it?
- There should be a named person in the school to whom the pupil can refer any difficulties. Many pupils, particularly those with ASD, may not otherwise bring any problems to the attention of staff. In some cases a regular time will need to be arranged when ICT support can be discussed.

All the pupils described in this chapter are attending mainstream primary and secondary schools and have a medical diagnosis of either ASD or an associated condition. Whilst most have statements of SEN and some learning difficulties associated with ASD, others have spent much of their education with unidentified difficulties. Dermot, for example, was not identified as having Asperger's syndrome until he was at secondary school.

Karl

Karl was first seen when in year six at primary school. He has a severe delay in communication, in the understanding of both external and internal language, with cognitive functions at around the eighteen-month developmental stage. He does produce some sounds but has no discernible speech. Karl understands some simple instructions and recognises his name when spoken.

Karl is obsessed with 'writing', and constantly wants to do this rather than any other activities, although he only makes random marks on paper. His level of participation usually consists of being present and aware of an activity (National Curriculum level P1). Sometimes he will gesture towards an object or activity to show that he wants to participate, or that he wants the activity to continue.

Barriers to curriculum access

The special educational provision set out in Karl's statement of SEN covers the areas of:

- communication;
- self-awareness;
- self-motivation.

Karl was first seen at the Learning Support Centre, which he found very unsettling, as he was not familiar with the setting. After about half an hour he was willing to sit with other pupils and observe the activity going on. His interest level was gauged by his attention to the activity and by eye contact and gestures indicating that he wanted to carry on with a particular activity.

The reward animations in most switch operated programs did not seem to interest him although he did seem to be paying some attention to the Blob program (Widgit Software). He was more interested in the nursery rhyme activities in the Speaking for Myself program (Topologika Software). He listened to these and indicated by pointing that he wanted to hear some of them again. He was quiet and paid attention for several minutes.

Karl also displayed some interest in a Powerpoint presentation that had been devised for another pupil. This consisted of photographs of some pupils at a secondary school, accompanied by recordings of speech introducing themselves. With help, Karl was able and willing to click the mouse button to advance through the slides.

Initial support

- Simple switch programs with colourful rewards accompanied by music were used to develop Karl's ability to focus on the computer screen. Programs incorporating nursery rhymes, whilst not age-appropriate, were also found to be the best way to engage his interest and provide a starting point for computer use.
- ICT support was then used to assist Karl's transition to secondary school. A simple switch operated program featuring photographs of new staff and other pupils at the new school was set up for Karl towards the end of the summer term and continued when he started secondary school. Staff working with Karl felt that he did respond to the photographs and that the program did help the transition process.
- A similar program featuring Karl undertaking different activities seemed to facilitate his understanding of the structure of the school day.

Karl will benefit from the continued use of ICT to support the development of basic cognitive skills and concepts and to assist his understanding of regular events and routines.

He will need continued support to access a computer, with switches providing the main means for access for the foreseeable future. The use of individually prepared switch operated programs was particularly relevant for Karl. These featured photographs of key staff and some other pupils. It sometimes seems that pupils on the autistic continuum often respond more positively to photographs of people than to the people themselves! This can theoretically be used to develop awareness of others and is a technique that we use quite often. Karl attended to the photographs on the computer for significantly longer than to the real people. He seemed to prefer the computer images and seemed almost to relate to some individuals through this medium. It is to be hoped that this later transfers more to the actual people! Sound was included so that they spoke to him as the switch was pressed.

The program used to make these was HyperStudio (TAG), but there are several other programs that can be used to make customised switch operated activities, such as SwitchIt! Maker and ChooseIt! Maker from Inclusive Technology. Microsoft Powerpoint and more sophisticated multimedia authoring software can also be used, but these may not allow for switch operation.

Karl often responds more to the sounds than to the visual content of a piece of software. This is quite often the case with pupils at a very early developmental stage and the use of multimedia programs with music and singing and other sound effects can be very helpful in maintaining attention and assisting the development of language and basic concepts. There are many early learning programs available with a variety of activities in a multimedia format. Several can be accessed using switches.

Communication and language are mentioned in Karl's statement as his main area of need, and ICT can support this by use of specific early learning software featuring simple spoken language.

Although it is usually desirable for pupils to use programs with age appropriate content and format, the nursery rhymes were very motivating for Karl and he responded strongly, requesting repeats by pointing towards the screen. Paired activities with other pupils taking turns and encouraging him to press the switch for repeat were also successful on occasion.

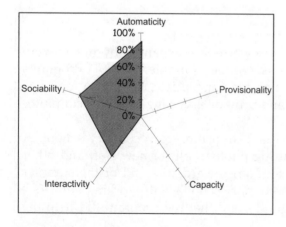

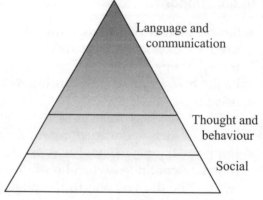

Figure 5.1 Qualities of ICT – Karl   **Figure 5.2** ASD Profile – Karl

Farzana

Farzana is a year one pupil and has ASD with severe learning difficulties. She has no speech and seems to have very limited receptive language.

She does not use any gestures or signs, but will lead adults to an activity she wants to do.

Farzana is a cheerful girl who shows a preference for adults she knows and will make sustained eye contact, particularly with members of her family and familiar staff.

Barriers to curriculum access

Farzana's statement specifies the need for alternative means of curriculum access and learning.

Farzana loves computers and will use the one in class at every opportunity. She always wants to use the SwitchIt! Patterns program with a big switch, which she presses continually. She glances briefly at the pattern effects and seems to enjoy them. However she doesn't spend long looking but keeps pressing the switch.

It is possible that Farzana has acquired the concept of cause and effect, but will at present use only a single switch and the same program, and it is hard to judge how much she understands.

When shown two other switch operated programmes – Blob and Spot on Games – she showed little interest, looking away from the screen and needing prompting and hand over hand assistance to press the switch. Apparently this is Farzana's usual reaction to unfamiliar activity; she much prefers those with which she is familiar.

When presented with two switches Farzana continued to press only the one on her right unless her hand was placed on the other switch. She seemed not to register that she could use two instead of one. She was also reluctant to continue.

When shown a tracker ball and the Touch Balloons program she again displayed no interest in it.

Initial support

- Initial support was aimed at encouraging Farzana to further develop single switch use – Spot on Games to develop anticipation and timing skills and to sustain her attention on the screen for longer periods of time.
- It may then be possible to develop the use of two switches to scan and select from a choice of items.
- Farzana was then encouraged to use a tracker ball, initially with the SwitchIt! Patterns program with which she was familiar and with simple games such as the Touch Games, Touch Balloons and other simple cause and effect programmes that can be used with a tracker ball to set up the cause and effect.

  As yet she has not understood the function of the tracker ball and much prefers to use the switch.

It was very difficult to engage Farzana in developmental activities leading to progression, due to her reluctance to engage in anything unfamiliar. This means that it was not possible to assess whether a particular activity would be of benefit for her after only a few sessions. It was necessary to try the new program or equipment on a regular basis until she accepted it, and then make an assessment of its efficacy.

This lack of interest in unfamiliar programs is not uncommon amongst pupils on the autistic spectrum and a similar procedure of regular exposure should be undertaken with such children before a decision can be made as to the degree of understanding and involvement the pupils may develop. She also found it difficult to sustain attention on any one activity (apart from the Patterns program), and would need frequent breaks to pursue her favourite activities.

Although the aim was to introduce the concept of choice through the use of two switches and appropriate programmes, Farzana has as yet not progressed to this. It may be that if her use of the tracker ball is successful this could be used as a means of making choices. If neither of these is successful single switch scanning techniques will be tried.

It can be seen from Figures 5.3 and 5.4 that the qualities of ICT relevant to Farzana at present are those of automaticity and interactivity. She does not seem to be any more likely to interact with others whilst using a computer than at other times, despite sustained attempts to use it as a means of working with others. The functions of provisionality and capacity are not yet relevant.

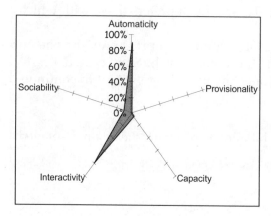

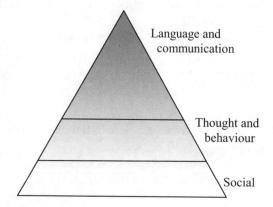

Figure 5.3 Qualities of ICT – Farzana   **Figure 5.4** ASD Profile – Farzana

Eric

Eric is in year four at primary school and has been described as being on the autistic continuum. He has a severe speech and language communication difficulty, with difficulty in processing verbal instructions and very limited expressive language, but his underlying understanding is in advance of these skills.

He has a need for activities to be always presented in same way.

His preferred learning style is visual/tactile.

Eric has a short attention span, but will attend to a computer for up to 30 minutes.

Barriers to curriculum access

Language, literacy, social skills and understanding, attention span and generalisation are the main areas of difficulty.

He has difficulty tolerating adults.

Eric is keen to use computers and accesses them by using the mouse to click on any part of the screen that interests him. He seems to want to identify and investigate anything that looks as if it will have an effect. He is therefore using the computer to set up cause and effect responses, with learning seemingly incidental. He does not use the keyboard for input.

There are several activities that he likes and will engage in for up to ten minutes. These are the My World programs, Dazzle drawing program and the Animated Alphabet. He will quickly close any program he does not like unless the mouse is removed from his grasp.

He uses the Talking Animated Alphabet and is able to match letters and select odd letters out by following the verbal instructions given.

Initial support

- The Talking Write Away program (BlackCat) with word grids was used to develop Eric's ability to match words to clip art pictures, or names to the Oxford Reading Tree characters. This will ideally provide a basis for future development and progression.
- The Inclusive Writer program, which generates symbols matched to the words input, was used as a means of curriculum access in general for Eric. It was used for activities such as labelling, matching and sequencing across all subject areas and also for matching names to photographs of people.
- Speech feedback is used with both the above programs to reinforce his sight vocabulary and provide auditory reinforcement. It is hoped that he will develop error identification and self-correction skills in the future by using the speech to check words.
- A concept keyboard was used to introduce the concept of an input device other than the mouse that had been Eric's sole means of access to the computer. Eric was willing to use it to type in his name and the letters of the alphabet.

  It was used for simple matching activities initially, or single words such as Eric's name.
- The Startwrite program, which enables text input to be printed in dotted fonts for over-writing, might help to motivate Eric to attempt more writing by hand in the future.

Eric is representative of many children with autism in his preference for exploring the computer primarily by mouse, often ignoring the keyboard altogether. These pupils may move very rapidly through activities, often without seeming to spend sufficient time to process information or understand activities. They quickly discover how to close programs and may do so even if requested not to. Their use of the mouse can be too quick to prevent this, and dual mouse control through a mouse splitter device can be used to moderate their speed and control.

These pupils often seem to be using the computer as a simple cause and effect device and may show little interest in staying on any activity for more than a few minutes. Their learning from programs is therefore incidental and fragmented rather than structured and cumulative.

In order to overcome this it is necessary to find their favourite activity, or one on which they can sustain attention for a relatively long period, and work out ways of extending this. In Eric's case this was the ORT talking stories and clip art (Sherston Software). He had begun to show an interest in the stories in class, would memorise some of them and point to individual names in the text. The talking stories enabled him to work through the books at his own pace and click on individual words, thus reinforcing his sight vocabulary. The use of the clip art in TWAW, combined with character names in a word list, introduced this function of the program and set the basis for development. Other programs with grids, such as Clicker (Crick Software Ltd), could also be used. When the clip art was used with the Startwrite program, Eric was able to label the characters and print out the work with dotted fonts. He then traced over these to produce handwritten class work. This served to increase his motivation to engage in writing, which he had previously been reluctant to undertake.

It is also important to introduce a means of input that will lead to use of a keyboard, if possible. An Intellikeys overlay keyboard (Inclusive Technology) was provided, which had a choice of simplified keyboard layouts, all in large high contrast lower case layout. This engaged Eric's attention immediately and he began to use it without prompting.

The board was also programmed with simple literacy activities for Eric, such as typing his name from a small selection of letters, constructing simple phrases, etc. Speech feedback from the Talking Write Away reinforced the language structure.

Inclusion was promoted by the use of subjects and materials that related directly to those used in class and using the computer to produce materials that Eric could use in class, such as the Startwrite, Oxford Reading Tree and Inclusive Writer materials.

Future objectives for ICT support would include progression in all the areas above, plus the introduction of paired activities on the computer.

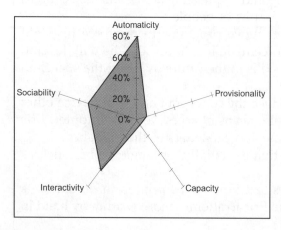

Figure 5.5 Qualities of ICT – Eric

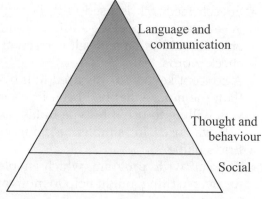

Figure 5.6 ASD Profile – Eric

Derick

Derick was first encountered whilst in year four at primary school. At that time he was working towards level one of the National Curriculum in all subject areas. He had major difficulties in the area of language and communication.

It was recommended that he use several early literacy programmes in order to develop his language and literacy skills. He used these to reinforce literacy and early learning activities for several months and became particularly keen on the Talking Animated Alphabet to the extent that he refused to use other programmes when this program was in sight. The box had to be hidden from his view until he had completed other tasks.

An opportunity then arose for Derick and another pupil to participate in the 1999/2000 BECTa project on speech recognition and SEN. This project researched how such software could assist pupils with a range of special educational needs. This part of the project was particularly interesting as it was the only centre working with children with autistic spectrum disorders.

An early speech recognition program was used (Dragon Dictate Classic). This recognised each word as it was spoken – discrete speech recognition. It is necessary for each user to train the program to recognise their speech patterns and pronunciation. This is achieved by training set words to begin with. The numbers between one and twenty were used with Derick, who was able to recognise each number and speak it reasonably clearly. An advantage of a discrete recognition program is that it will accept a noticeable mispronunciation as long as it is consistent. For example, Derick pronounced 'orange' as 'ran-he', but as this was a consistent pronunciation it was possible to train the program to recognise this as the word 'orange' and produce the correctly spelled word.

Once initial training was complete the program was trained with the words Derick was learning as part of his literacy targets. The training was achieved by showing pictures and Derick speaking the word. Several sessions were required to achieve recognition and Derick was surprisingly tolerant and cooperative in what was an extremely repetitive activity.

Once the training of the words was complete they were used as a learning activity. Derick would be presented with an on screen clip art picture and separate flashcard of the word, which he would then speak into the microphone. He would match the text that appeared under the picture with the flashcard to see if the word was spelled correctly. If it was incorrect he would delete it and try again. Derick seemed to enjoy this and was always a willing participant for fifteen to twenty minutes. When he had 'had enough' of this he would often issue a piercing scream – his signal that it was time to stop.

This unusual use of a speech recognition program provided Derick with an additional means of curriculum access in the area of language and literacy development.

This case illustrates that programs that may at first seem of little use to particular pupils can sometimes be adapted and used sucessfully to address individual needs by providing alternative means of delivering the curriculum. This can be particularly valuable for pupils whose progress is slow and who may need to have the same task presented in a hundred and one different ways over a long period of time!

Whilst the project was deemed to be a success in terms of the effect on learning and the introduction of a new way of addressing a task, there were concerns about the use of voice recognition in this way for some ASD pupils. This mainly concerned the possible effect on Derick's persistent echolalia. Whilst there was no noticeable impact on this, it was felt that the practice of whispering the word for him to repeat during the training might encourage echolalia. For this reason the use of flashcard and picture prompts was maximised and the words spoken to him only if absolutely necessary.

In the case study above the qualities of ICT most relevant were those of provisionality and automaticity, which allowed Derick to speak the words and have them generated on screen immediately, and to delete any that were incorrect.

The quality of sociability was also evident in Derick's shared understanding of the activity with his support teacher, ability to follow instructions and cooperate in the initial training of the program. Interactivity was demonstrated by the program responding to the words spoken by Derick and his response to what appeared on the screen.

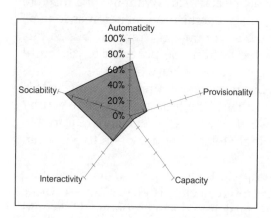

Figure 5.7 Qualities of ICT – Derick

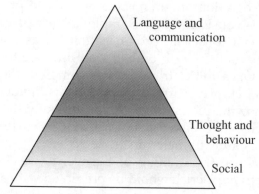

Figure 5.8 ASD Profile – Derick

Mark

Mark was first seen when he was in year six at primary school. Although he was achieving at level one or two of the National Curriculum, Mark had good literacy skills, being able to read simple texts and produce short pieces of writing independently.

Barriers to curriculum access

School staff were concerned that Mark's need for consistency and perfection in his written work was becoming a barrier to learning. He would redraft a piece of work every time he made a mistake, tear up work he considered unacceptable and sometimes fly into a rage if prevented from doing this. He rarely completed work.

Mark loves computers and used an Acorn computer at school. When I first met Mark he was typing a record of events for his diary, which he did every day. He seemed to be a competent user of simple word processors. He was able to change font size, and style, enter and edit text.

It was clear that Mark was familiar with the task and always used the same layout, font and size.

In his classroom Mark used a PC with the primary toolbox.

When shown a portable machine (Dreamwriter IT), Mark was very interested. He quickly worked out how to use the trackpad and opened pocket Word without prompting. He was then asked to type in a short poem that the class had worked on previously.

This proved more problematic than expected: Mark changed the font size several times, then discovered that his preferred font was not available on that machine. He was very unhappy about this and took some persuading to do the work in an alternative font. Mark decided that he wanted to centre the poem on the page, but tried to do this using the space bar. He could not be persuaded that the centre justification would achieve this. He deleted and re-typed the first few lines several times. There was no apparent reason for this.

Mark did eventually finish the piece, but needed much prompting to carry on rather than constantly edit and re-edit.

It seemed that the use of a portable might not address Mark's need for perfection, but could in fact reinforce it. It was decided to let Mark use the portable on a trial basis in order for staff to make a better assessment of its support potential.

After a few weeks they concluded that the portable was unsuitable for Mark, as it did not diminish his perfectionism. They were also concerned that his monopoly of the machine and refusal to work with others on it could be detrimental to his social skills and would not promote inclusion.

A similar procedure occurred when Mark was in year seven at secondary school. Staff observed his fixation with perfection and considered the use of a portable. After some discussion and observation of him doing his work on a computer they reached the same conclusion as the primary staff.

Mark is now in year eight and uses the school computers regularly for word processing his work and as a reward or occasionally a 'time out' activity.

This provides a very good example of how the obvious and ideal solution to a pupil's difficulties can turn out to be anything but ideal!

In Mark's case the portable word processor simply provided another means to perpetuate his habit of correcting, deleting and striving for perfection, whilst also isolating him from peers and teachers, as he would not communicate with others whilst using the computer or allow others to touch the machine.

His primary school support staff felt that there was also a real danger that Mark would damage the machine if he became frustrated. Although the frequency of his rages was and is diminishing, Mark is prone to quite violent rages during which he may throw or damage things.

This underlines the importance of trying out and monitoring interventions very closely whilst taking a broad view of the impact on the pupil's education. It is quite possible that, whilst a portable could be of benefit to a pupil in carrying out work, the overall impact in terms of inclusion and participation could be detrimental. In cases such as this the decision on whether or not to carry on with the support should be taken after discussion with all concerned: parents, school staff and the pupil.

Even if a support package is deemed to be effective and successful it is still vital to have monitoring in place to pick up any changes in the suitability of equipment and software, changes in the needs of the pupils and progression.

Support should ideally be formally reviewed at least once a year and adjusted as and when necessary.

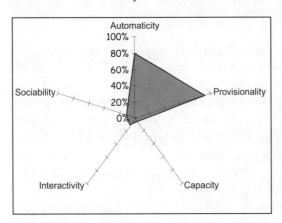

Figure 5.9 Qualities of ICT – Mark

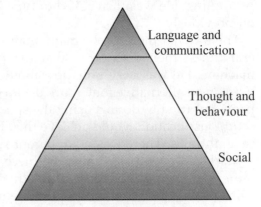

Figure 5.10 ASD Profile – Mark

Dermot

Dermot has difficulties associated with Asperger's syndrome. He is now in year eight and was first assessed for ICT support when in year six. He was loaned some spelling software to support a multi-sensory literacy programme. His needs were re-assessed at the end of year seven at secondary school, as detailed below.

Dermot is extremely knowledgeable about subjects in which he has an interest and has a wide vocabulary of specialist terms.

Barriers to curriculum access

- mild learning difficulties;
- spelling difficulties;
- difficulty with control in handwriting;
- difficulty in understanding abstract concepts.

Dermot feels that too much is made of his style of writing and that the fact that it is legible is sufficient. He did however agree that his writing had improved markedly over the last few months, and perhaps this was a good thing. He had not considered using a word processor for schoolwork but does produce homework on the family computer.

Dermot typed fairly quickly using one finger on each hand. He has good knowledge of the keyboard and other functions. He knew how to open, save, print and exit the file.

Initial Support

- Dermot was allocated a portable word processor to use for *some* of his school-work. The use of this was built up gradually; initially it was used for a few subjects that involve a lot of writing, such as English and History.
- Samples of Dermot's handwriting show a considerable improvement over the space of six months. His letters are smaller, more consistent in size and consequently more legible. Whilst he clearly has motor and organisational difficulties it seems that there is still scope for development and consequently he should continue to write by hand for some of his lessons, particularly those that do not involve a great deal of writing. He could then concentrate on quality rather than quantity.
- Dermot may also benefit from the use of a touch-typing program in order to develop further his keyboard skills. There may be one available at the school by September; otherwise one can be provided. School staff will need to take account of Dermot's educational priorities in deciding if and when this could be practised. Ten to fifteen minutes practice at least three times a week should be sufficient for progress to be made.
- It seems from the text produced during the assessment that the vast majority of spelling errors will be picked up by a spellchecker and corrected easily by Dermot. He is also following the Phonological Awareness Training program during individual support sessions. The Wordshark program (Whitespace) could be used as necessary to reinforce the words he is working on. This program is available at the school.

This example shows that the perceived ideal support may not be workable, often for unforeseen reasons and sometimes for no discernable reason at all! In Dermot's case there was a clear benefit in the use of a portable. He was able to improve both the quality and quantity of schoolwork through its use, as can be seen in the examples of his handwritten and typed work (Figure 5.13). He was very pleased with the machine when he first received it and used it regularly.

At this point the situation seemed very positive with appropriate support in place, as perceived by all adults involved! Unfortunately this ideal situation did not continue: Dermot ceased to use the portable. At first he reported that he did not like carrying two bags. This problem was addressed by re-arranging his rucksack to accommodate the portable in addition to his books. He also did not like to spend time setting it up in lessons, saying that opening a book is much easier, a point that cannot be disputed!

Dermot also had concerns about security and responsibility for what he perceived to be a valuable piece of equipment. Pupils often have such concerns, and they can be difficult to address. In this case a safe place was found for Dermot to leave the portable when not using it. We looked at his timetable to identify blocks of lessons when it could and could not be used.

We also discussed the reaction of other pupils in wanting to see and use his machine. He found this particularly stressful and it is a problem with which staff cannot always help. The onus was on Dermot to deal with this, and various possible strategies were discussed with him. Despite this his worries did not abate, perhaps due to his limited social skills and range of strategies in dealing with other pupils.

A Psion Revo palmtop was then tried, but despite saying that he liked it Dermot would not use it and was not prepared to discuss the reasons for this. He has now been told that a portable can be provided for him if and when he feels comfortable using one, and this is how the situation remains.

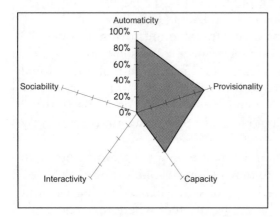

Figure 5.11 Qualities of ICT – Dermot

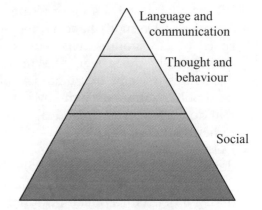

Figure 5.12 ASD Profile – Dermot

Printout 1, uncorrected

Hello my name is dermot. I am going to tell you about my cats. One is called tiger. I will tell you about him. He is a very nervos cat and I know that he hates ice. He will go mad if he touches it. He will hiss and spit at it then he tried to dissembowell it. He has a speshal need. It is called Cerabellum displasia. It means he is a bit clumsy. He's always falling off walls.

Dermot – Printout 2, corrected

Hello my name is Dermot. I am going to tell you about my cats. One is called tiger. I will tell you about him. He is a very nervous cat and I know that he hates ice. He will go mad if he touches it. He will hiss and spit at it then he tried to disembowel it. He has a special need. It is called Cerebellum displasia. It means he is a bit clumsy. He's always falling off walls.

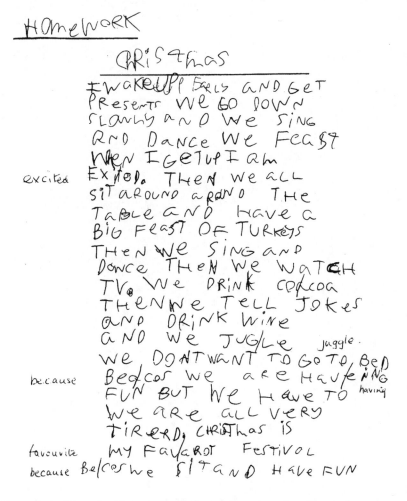

Figure 5.13 Samples of handwritten and word processed work – Dermot

6 Early learning, computing and communication

The object of this chapter is to examine early computer use for children with ASD. We will try to offer practical advice on what to look for in children, how to encourage and help and the stages through which most children with ASD pass in early computer use. The term 'early learning' rather than 'early years' has been used to cover both younger children and those who are older, and possibly with more severe and profound learning difficulties, but who have had little or no contact with computers. Communication has been included in this chapter as communication opportunities between the child and teacher, carer or peers are often facilitated by the less threatening focus of attention on the computer screen and the motivation provided by a shared interest in the activity.

In the opening chapter of this book we suggested that inappropriate or stressful adult intervention in ICT use for children with autism could not only be unproductive but might even deter the child from future computer use. The opening section of this chapter hopes to outline some practical 'dos' and 'don'ts' when introducing the child with autism to computers.

We will start from the most basic computer use. For an older, more able pupil, you may want to skip the first part of this chapter.

Is the child ready to use a computer?

This question probably applies to a young child, or an older child who has had little or no previous computer experience and may have quite severe special needs.

The first thing to look for is *intentional behaviour*, that is movements or language that are clearly deliberately, rather than randomly, produced by the child. Consider the checklist in Figure 6.1; if the majority of your ticks are in the *intentional* side of the list then the child is ready for computer use.

What do I do if he or she is not ready?

Even if the child does not appear to be ready for computer use at the moment, they may develop and change and it is important to offer them exposure to and experience of computer use. In terms of the new QCA 'P' scales framework this would be classed as an 'encounter' and although initially this may have no obvious learning outcome, for some pupils, 'their willingness to tolerate a shared activity' may, in itself, be significant. (National Curriculum, 2001)

Is the standard computer suitable for the child?

Many children, even very young ones, show a surprising ability to cope with the type of standard office set-up shown here. But this cannot be assumed for the child with ASD. One or more of the components may present barriers to use (Figure 6.2).

Checklist of Intentional Behaviour

Pre-intentional Behaviour	Intentional Behaviour
1. Sucking	1. Smiling in response
2. Crying	2. Laughter
3. Dribbling	3. Reaching out
4. Rooting	4. Changing crying tone to gain attention
5. Facial movements	5. Simple body gesture
6. Startled by a loud noise	6. Breathing patterns
7. Body reflexes	7. Vocalisation
8. Tongue movement	8. To and fro vocalisations
9. Unfocused looking around	9. Focus on object
	10. Tracking moving object
	11. Making eye contact with person

(based upon chart prepared by Lorna Flowers and others, LBN)

Figure 6.1 Checklist of intentional behaviour

Figure 6.2 The standard computer set-up

Potential barriers for child with ASD

1. Frustration due to the complexity and clutter of the QWERTY keyboard.
2. Fine motor control and coordination is required for mouse operation.

3. Simultaneous attention to mouse and screen can be difficult.

4. Some pupils with ASD have an obsession with leads, wires and string.

5. The processor with its drives, slots,

Solutions to try

1. Try alternative keyboards, 'Bigkeys', concept keyboard, switches etc.
2. Try 'mini' size mouse, tracker ball, joystick, switches etc. Adjust mouse settings, speed, etc. from 'Settings'.
3. Improve association by sticking tactile picture of screen cursor on mouse button.
4. Cover, conceal and fix down as far as possible. Laptops, etc. have no leads. Infrared ports eliminate leads.
5. Cover, conceal in box or cupboard or even in another room.
6. Cover, conceal, etc. or just turn it round so switch cannot be seen.
7. Adjust screen 'Settings'. Laptop screens may be preferred. Screen guards may help. Consider reflection from windows, fluorescent lights etc.
8. Adjust/turn off sound settings. Earphones reduce room distractions.
9. Distance or conceal printer. Use examples of finished work as 'carrot' to persuade child to be patient.

University of Wales, Newport
Prifysgol Cymru, Casnewydd
Library Services

User ID: B20301979

Title: Changing attitudes to punishment public
opinion
Author: Roberts, Julian V.
Item ID: 1933022
Date due: 31/1/2011,23:59

Title: Getting services for your child on the au
tism spe
Author: Foley, Matthew G.
Item ID: 1826146
Date due: 31/1/2011,23:59

Title: Autism and ICT : a guide for teachers & p
arents
Author: Hardy, Colin
Item ID: 1826408
Date due: 31/1/2011,23:59

To renew online please go to
the Library web page
or you can phone the libraries
llt-yr-yn 01633 432310
aerleon 01633 432294

... may result in frustration and anger for the user and ... computer use.

... ost basic level can only start when the child has knowl- ... person who can impact upon the world and the people

... 'agent of change'

... ecipients of communication, seldom initiating interaction ... hods of attracting the attention of others the use of crude ... ing, tugging of clothing and so on. Worse still, violent or ... be perceived as the only means to gain attention or alter the course of events... hope with ICT and other forms of augmentative communication is to offer the child alternative and varied responses in relating to and communicating with the world around them.

Switches and the 'cause and effect' relationship

The object of switch operation early on is to establish and consolidate the so-called 'cause and effect' relationship. This is the relationship between deliberate actions by the child and the realisation that these can have an impact or controlling influence on the world around them.

Establishing the 'cause and effect' relationship

Early on you may well find that music or sound of some kind is the most motivating 'effect'. A simple circuit, including a switch in a 'loop' to activate a bell, buzzer or other device, is simple to construct. Such circuits can be powered by a low voltage battery and are therefore safe for child use. This is a useful facility as the child with ASD is often fascinated by technical devices and keen to investigate, dismantle and experiment with them.

Switches

There are lots of different switches. One can probably be bought or made to suit your child. They do not have to be connected to a computer. Room lighting switches, the 'green person' button on a pedestrian crossing, and the bell push on a bus are all types of switches. The *control* that they exert can be a very addictive feature and make their use highly motivating for children and others. The touch sensitive screen may be the most obvious method of response for the child whose focus of attention is, anyway, the screen.

Figure 6.3 Switches

Switch operated toys are increasingly becoming available at a reasonable price. When buying cheap battery operated toys in markets or discount stores, look to see if they have a 'jack plug' socket, which means you can attach a switch (like an earphone socket, you can spot some in Figure 6.4). In addition, a large number of toys can be quite simply adapted for switch use with battery switch adaptors (Inclusive Technology). Again as long as the toy is battery operated there is little danger for the inquisitive child. Such toys can be chosen to reflect the interest of the child and often combining movement and sound can prove very appealing.

Simple switch programs for the computer

The best way to get a feel of a switch program is to try one for yourself. Good switch programs are very addictive and not just for young children! Try one of the 'Switch On' series for example 'Switch On Zoo' (Brilliant Computing). Try to find a program that reflects the interests of the child; for those with ASD the following spring to mind: 'Switchit! Diggers' and Switchit! Gadgets' (Inclusive Technology), 'Switch On Transport' (Brilliant Computing). You can even make up your own simple switch programs to more closely mirror the child's preoccupations and interests, see for example, 'Switchit! Maker' (Inclusive Technology). Similarly, there are a wide range of switches available in the catalogues.

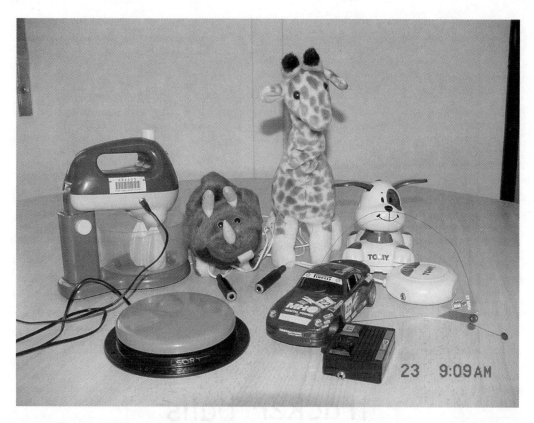

Figure 6.4 Switch operated toys (Note the jack plug sockets on some of the toys. The giraffe and prehistoric monster have had their batteries adapted and leads with jack plugs attached. The food mixer has a switch attached to its jack plug.)

Developing switch operation

1. Early on success is essential, as this will assure the child that they can exert control by use of the switch. Technical or other failures may de-motivate the child from any further ICT use. Take advantage of any random movement of hand, head etc. and hold the switch so close that this is sure to activate the switch. Later the child will begin to realise that this movement is activating the switch, establishing and reinforcing the cause and effect relationship.
2. Pressing the switch at the right time is the important next step. Early switch use tends to be random and often frenetic. It is important to move the child on from this to a more controlled and selective use of the switch only when it is required to achieve the desired affect.
3. Making choices with switches is the ultimate goal of switch use, where either on screen or on a communication device, the child is making active choices between one or more choices, for example words on screen, 'drink', 'toilet', 'food'. . . This may involve the use of one or more switches and scanning grids, which leads us into a discussion of alternative and augmentative communication later in this chapter.

The Inclusive Technology website has some useful articles and information on switches and switch software appropriate for a range of ages. Other alternative access devices described in the next chapter can include:

- concept keyboards;
- alternative keyboards;
- key-guards;
- tracker ball and joystick;
- voice recognition.

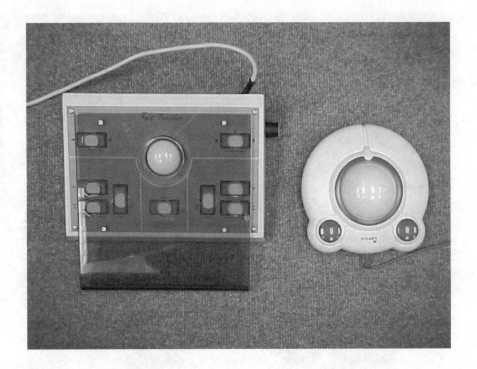

tracker balls

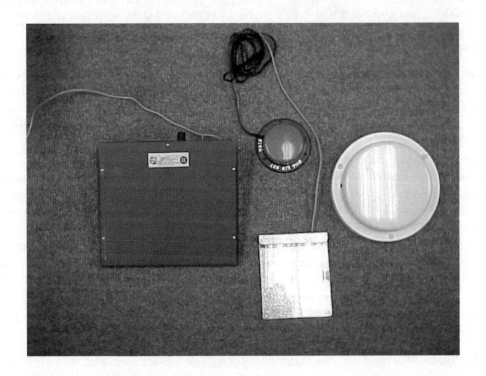

switches

Figure 6.5 Alternative access

Stages in computer use for the child with ASD

Practical experience suggests that there are a number of stages through which children with ASD pass in making use of computers. These are described in the following charts along with some tips for useful intervention at each stage.

Stage 1. The play stage

Child focus	Helper focus
It is important to let the child go through a stage of play. There is a need for the child to get to feel at ease with the computer and learn its calming and controllable aspects and this is particularly the case for non-verbal children (Murray 1997). Children will often sit for long periods of time repeating the same operation, for example copying and pasting the same item time and again onto a screen in 'My World' (Granada Software). Let them go through this stage only changing the program when they are clearly losing interest. Programs that contain images that are known to be of interest to the child, trucks, cars, volcanoes, dinosaurs and so on, will be appreciated. The child may be willing to have a companion sit with them as long as the computer is the centre of attention.	Observe and learn about the child and how they are interacting with the computer. As adults we will need to 'let go' and relinquish our role as director of operations. Sit beside, but do not crowd, the child. Offer advice only when requested or when needed to avoid frustration. But as Murray (1997, p. 101) points out 'that phase of exploration and discovery can be an ideal basis for communication with a sensitive helper'. You do not need to be an ICT expert, but confidence and familiarity with software and hardware helps. Most important, share with the child the excitement at experimenting with ICT. Set up the uninterrupted access times so that the sessions are not marred by other important things such as lunchtime, home time or even bed time.

Software to try

- Simple art or paint programs have been found to be good introductions to computers e.g. 'Paint' in Windows, Accessories.
- Any program that motivates or interest the child will do, for example the switch programs already mentioned here, 'Switchit! Diggers' and Switchit! Gadgets' (Inclusive Technology), for example 'Blob' (Inclusive Technology).
- My World (Granada) has also proved useful. Depending on age, try the screen 'My World Dress Teddy', or try a screen that relates to personal interests, dinosaurs, volcanoes etc.
- You may be able to get away with software that is not age appropriate, but software that is too difficult or demanding will almost certainly lead to anger and frustration. It may even discourage future ICT use.
- Games programs are the most commonly purchased for home use and so may be a familiar and motivating starting point. What programs you choose and how you use them is crucial for the child who has 'got to win'. It may be better to compete against oneself than others.
- Resist the temptation to use formal educational programs too early.

Example from a nursery

An example of how one nursery developed this 'play stage' was reported in the journal *Young Children*, March 2000. This article, 'Computers in a Developmentally Appropriate Curriculum', by Genan T. Anderson, tells of a young boy's first encounters with computers. Creig was motivated to explore the keyboard through the software 'Bailey's Book House'. He was partnered at the computer with a peer and there were times when both children would try to assert their authority over the use of the mouse. However, within six weeks, Creig was proficient at using the program correctly. What is of more importance is the way in which other developments took place after Creig encountered computers. Another child initiated a play situation with Creig immediately after he had finished a computer session and instead of his usual negative response, the staff were amazed to see him complying. 'Because the cooperative computer interaction and the ensuing role play followed each other so close in time, to us there seemed a direct connection.' (Genan T. Anderson, p. 92, March 2000) From the early 'play stage' Creig had progressed to developing a relationship both with computers and with peers.

The play stage: observation sheet

Focus	Comment
How is the pupil sitting/ standing in relation to the computer?	
Is the pupil attracted to the sound?	
Are there certain visual elements to the pro- grammes, which always attract him/her?	
How does the pupil use the mouse?	
Will the pupil tolerate others in close proximity?	
Does the pupil insist on controlling the mouse all of the time?	
Comment on the pupil's reaction to what is happening:	

Planning next steps
1)
2)
3)
4)

Stage 2. Developing a relationship

Chiid focus	Helper focus
Experiment with a wider range of programs and increasingly try to draw the child into these choices. Participation with others and even turn taking may increase along with a shared interest and enthusiasm for computing. Self-esteem can be boosted where the child is encouraged to take on the role of 'helper', setting up programs, keeping scores and attending to minor faults.	Provide help and an interested commentary while observing the child. As the child gets to like the computer and becomes accustomed to your presence trust can be built up and along with this your relationship with the child. There will increasingly be communication opportunities for both you and other adults and children around the computer. Modelling an activity by the helper or support teacher can often be a good way to present new programs or aspects of programs to the child. Structure sessions so that increasingly choices are directed towards the classroom curriculum, for example a CD encyclopaedia or atlas with relevant information, a 'Clicker Grid' loaded with information for French and so on.

Software to try

- Interactive programs help the child to learn 'turn taking', initially with the computer, but hopefully later with you and other children (Murray 1997).
- Simple modelling, simulation and adventure programs can be used to represent real or fantasy situations in a safe and structured way. This could include programs such as My World, talking books, e.g. Oxford Reading Tree (Sherston).
- Games programs are often frowned on in school particularly during lesson time. For the child with autism it may be worth finding time for their use. Games are endorsed within the National Curriculum (e.g. KS1, 5b the use of adventure games). The child with autism is often as good at games as others and will more readily accept the presence of others. Murray (1997, p. 105) suggests that as a result, 'the potential for peer group prestige, normalisation, and willing co-operation and communication is huge'.
- Open ended software such as 'Clicker' grids (Inclusive Technology), or talking word processors, e.g. Talking Write Away, can be customised to suit the ability and personal interests of individual children.
- A good supply of clip art and or images taken with a digital camera (or scanned from photos), again chosen to reflect pupil interest, is a good accompaniment to open ended software, e.g Oxford Reading Tree Clip Art (Sherston).

Developing a relationship: observation sheet

Focus	Comment
Will the pupil tolerate beginning and endings to his/her time on the computer?	
What is the pupil's reaction to turn taking with an adult or a peer?	
Note which programs are particularly motivating for your pupil.	
Is the pupil easily distracted whilst working on the computer or is he/she quite 'shut off' to the surroundings?	
If you intervene and disrupt the program, will the pupil indicate to you that they want you to help get it back etc.?	

Planning next steps
1)
2)
3)
4)

Stage 3. Independent user

Child focus	Helper focus
Some children will 'take off' in terms of computer use and become increasingly independent in setting up and using programs. Take advantage of this enthusiasm by introducing more powerful generic software such as word processor and desktop publishing programs. This is also the point at which it is safe to start introducing a range of 'pedagogic' or teaching software. Structure choices, as far as possible, to the relevant curriculum areas and key stage, but as far as possible, involve the child in these selections. Independent use of the computer should be encouraged and praised. Increasing complexity of communal activities may be possible, not least collaborative writing projects. Knowledge and trust of a group of adults and peers needs to have been built up around the computer.	Confidence and interest in computing may well result in the child being willing to accept increasing degrees of help from yourself or even from another and little known person who shares an interest in, and expertise in, computing. Increasingly your relationship with the child and that of the peer group will be more two way as you share a problem solving and investigative approach to computing. Up until now the child may well have been able to pick up most or all of their knowledge simply by observing other adults and children. Indeed many parents and carers are shocked by the computer skills of a child who has had no formal training. However research indicates that the deeper elements of more powerful programs such as word processors cannot be picked up in this fashion. In these cases direct teaching will be necessary.

Software to try

- More powerful generic software such as desktop publishers, spreadsheets, databases and presentation programs can be experimented with by the student, e.g. the word processor 'Word', the desk top publishing program 'Publisher', the spreadsheet Excel, 'Access' database and so on (all Microsoft).
- Teaching programs which practise specific elements of the curriculum, such as Wordshark (Inclusive Technology), can now be introduced.
- Integrated Learning Systems (ILS) such as SuccessMaker. The 'drill and practice' nature of this type of software may be demotivating for some students. For the child with ASD they may represent a more soothing and predictable learning environment, as part of a broader curriculum or at least as a retreat when under stress.

The independent user: observation sheet

Focus	Comment
Observe the pupil's routine and method of initiating computer sessions. Do not always be the one who directs the 'when and what'	
Note any preferences in relation to 'work buddies'. What are the pupil's reactions if these are changed or kept the same?	
What curriculum areas are adequately supported by relevant ICT programmes in your class?	
Make a 'wish list' of ICT software, which would link with the pupil's interests and cross over into curriculum areas.	

Follow up focus	Action taken and by whom	Date

Augmentative and alternative communication (AAC)

For the child who uses little or no speech or who has language and communication difficulties augmentative and alternative communication may well be worth investigating. It can cover a wide range of approaches, including gestures such as eye pointing, SIGNALONG and other signing systems, communication boards and books which may utilise photographs drawings or formal symbol systems such as Rebus.

ICT based solutions can include voice output communication aids (VOCAs) or similar communication software loaded on a computer. These involve the child touching a cell of a grid which leads to a sound (usually speech) being produced. The cell would have a pictorial cue on it to remind the child of the message, 'toilet', 'drink', 'walk' and so on, and these words would be spoken by the computer. In some cases a switch can activate the cell of a VOCA or the cell of a grid on a computer screen. The simplest form of VOCA is a single message switch such as the 'BIGmack'.

As far as is practical you may be able to paste or Blu-Tack real objects on to the cell or switch: a button for the message 'coat' for example, a cup handle for the message 'drink'.

The type of pictorial cues used can be critical

Some children with ASD will readily accept a symbol or picture as a generic representation, for example a symbol of a cup for any form of drink. Other children will need the actual object, e.g. the cup, as the cue that they will use to ask for a drink. Later they may accept a part of a cup, e.g. the handle, as the cue, or a photograph of the actual cup, scratches, chips and all. Later a drawing of a generic 'cup' or even a symbol for a cup may be substituted for photographs or real objects.

It is important to find out what level of symbolic representation, if any, is meaningful to a particular child with ASD and make sure that this is used in combination with whatever communication aid is chosen.

The road to symbolic representation

Augmentative and Alternative Communication (AAC)

Eye pointing	Voice Output Communication Aids (VOCAs)
Gesture	Synthesised (robotic) or Digitised (human)
Signing, Symbols	Static or Dynamic Display

Graphic	Voice Output	Comment
Actual Object	YOU speak when the child pushes the cup at you, "oh you want a drink"	Even this is a move in the right direction. The child is symbolically associating drinking with an object the cup.
Photograph	**drink**	For some children with ASD you will need the photograph of the actual cup, scratches and all! Use this in the VOCA as the prompt for the digitised or better the synthesised output, "drink".
Picture	**drink**	For some children, or later, a picture of a similar cup may do.
Symbol	**drink**	Later still you may be able to substitute a symbolic cup image for drink.
Text "drink"	**drink**	Text is the ultimate symbolic representation of an object.

Figure 6.6 The road to non-verbal communication

The 'BIGmack' switch is a good starting point. It is a stand alone large switch which is simple to program 'on the hoof' to record a single word, brief phrase, sentence or any other short burst of sound. It has the advantages of portability and immediacy in terms of recording and replaying something of interest and personal importance to the child and carers. Here are some suggestions:

- BIGmack programmed with simple message for child to take around school, e.g. to ask for dinner register, to give simple instruction to another child or adult, to ask for a pen, the football, tracing paper etc.
- Numeracy and literacy whole class sessions – communication aid programmed with simple responses for structured questioning by the teacher; for example, 'Yes', 'No', 'larger', 'smaller', the numbers 1–9, key words, etc.
- Numeracy and literacy plenary session message programmed into BIGmack by support staff or peer group as a means for child to report back their work.
- BIGmack can be programmed with repeated phrase from a story, the line of a song or poem etc. so that child can participate as whole class chant.
- The peer group program a communication aid with playground language for child's use. This can have amusing or even alarming results for parents and staff! It does however increase the street credibility of the focus child and of the communication device that is being used.

Figure 6.7 BIGmack

Little Ed (Granada Learning, Software Appendix) is a small, handheld VOCA which can be programmed for a range of static overlays. These give a variety of sizes of grids, 4, 8 and so on. Each cell can be programmed with one word or short message.

Other simple speech output devices include Tech/Talk8 and Tech/Speak32 (Inclusive Technology). Like BIGmack, Little Ed and Tech/Talk all share certain fundamentals which are probably more important to commutation aids than anything else. They are:

- simple to program;
- easy to use for children, parents and staff;
- robust;
- light and portable;
- relatively cheap and easily replaceable.

Figure 6.8 Simple speech output device

More complex communication devices can store a much larger number of messages. Instead of static cells, that is, cells that only play the message shown on them, they have dynamic cells. These cells can open up on screen a whole new range of choices. So for example a cell with the symbol for food, when pressed or activated, would open up a new set of cells each containing a different type of food and so on.

The advice of a speech and language therapist

The advice of a speech and language therapist is often useful when considering communication aids, for example in establishing whether the child has 'communicative intent'. Bear in mind that such a person may have little or no expertise in ICT. The therapist can offer insights on speech and language, the technician on ICT and the teacher on pedagogy and the child. Collaboration between these people can lead to exciting and imaginative results.

A specialist centre can be useful in that they have considerable experience of a whole range of devices and the assessment of an individual child's needs. For complex equipment it may be better to go to one site where a range of equipment and software can be conveniently tried.

However, bear in mind that communication by its very nature is not an activity performed in isolation. The successful operation of any communication aid is dependent not only upon the child feeling at ease and able to use it but similarly carers, teachers, support assistants and others with whom the child will be communicating. In the long run it will be they whom the child turns to for advice on how to work the device and for help when it goes wrong.

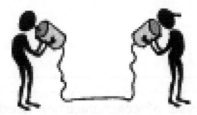

Figure 6.9 It takes two to tango

For any communication aid to achieve its purpose its use must be understood and supported not only by the child but also by all those adults and other children around the child. The whole environment in which the child operates needs to be considered if the communication aid is to work effectively. Some considerations are outlined in Figure 6.10.

Audit of Communication Need

To be completed by all those in regular contact with the pupil and by an advocate on behalf of the pupil. Please record examples of common or regular communication needs.

Pupil Name _____   Class or Tutor Group _____

Date & Time	Those Present	Place	Description of Communication • Who began the communication? • What was the message?
			Continue over

Analysis of communication need
- Are there common times or places where communication occurs?
- Who most often communicates to the pupil?
- Who does the pupil most often communicate with?
- What are the most common types of communication?

Informed choice of ICT set up and support

Figure 6.10 Audit of communication need

Microworlds

These are computer programs that on screen use objects, people and events which to some extent or another mimic the real world. The child is able to explore and experiment in this miniature world from the safety and security of their PC. The provisional qualities of ICT, described in Chapter 4, are important here in allowing the user to learn from mistakes and try again.

The word 'Microworld' is a very broad definition, which covers a wide range of different types of programs, some of which we describe briefly here:

- Talking books allow you to hear the whole story, time and time again, or go back to select individual words or phrases as many times as you like. Picture animations may also be included. Most reading schemes now have talking versions, see for example Oxford Reading Tree (Sherston), some can be switch operated or accessed by Intellikeys, see 'Living Books' (Inclusive Technology). Remember also that many reference CDs have animation and sound, and the facility to 'select' and play a section of text.
- 'My World' (Inclusive Technology, Granada Learning etc.) has already been described extensively here.
- Virtual Reality programs create simulations of real life or other situations and allow the user to participate in choices and challenges, but within the physical and psychological safety of the computer. Special helmets, goggles, input gloves, etc. may be supplied.
- Logo, popular in the 1980s, is a simple programming language that enables children to control a floor robot or turtle or on-screen movement of objects. It is this *control* that may be the attractive feature to some children with ASD and the need to think ahead one or more steps in the program may encourage more formal thinking.
- Modelling has much in common with virtual reality in that it simulates real situations and allows the user to pose questions 'What if I did this . . .?', 'Should I go this way or that way . . .?' and learn from the outcomes. See for example the 'Lifeskills' program for older learners in the Inclusive Technology catalogue, which places the user in a café, pub, post office etc. But equally programs like spreadsheets can be used to simulate mathematical or financial problems and, using simple formulae, view various outcomes.

Figure 6.11

7 Writing and recording

For many children with language and communication difficulties the blank sheet of paper is an impassable hurdle. In a school system obsessed by recording this becomes a major barrier to learning. Whether it is a story told to a year two class, a description of an event in a year five History class or a demonstration in a year nine Science lesson, there is the inevitable requirement to 'write about it'. In addition the vast majority of Standard Assessment Tests and GCSE exams are pencil and paper based. Learning support teachers and learning support assistants who assist children in these tasks, or parents trying to help their child do homework, must be familiar with a retort from the child along the lines of 'I don't know what to write'.

The act of writing is often broken down into two types of activity:

- The basic skills of transcription. The National Literacy Strategy (NLS) suggests that children should 'have fluent and legible handwriting'.
- The more complex skill of composition which can be further sub-divided for example by the NLS into:

    (i) planning;
    (ii) drafting;
    (iii) revising;
    (iv) editing.

ICT has a part to play in both transcription and composition. The distinction between transcription and composition will be used to anticipate barriers to learning for pupils with ASD and suggest suitable software and hardware to try.

1. Basic skills of transcription

I had the worst handwriting in my class. Many autistic children have problems with motor control in their hands. Neat handwriting is sometimes very hard. This can totally frustrate the child. To reduce frustration and help the child to enjoy writing, let him type on the computer. Typing is often much easier. (Grandin 2000b)

The National Curriculum (Inclusion Statement (C/3a) (QCA/DfEE 1999) makes it clear that it is perfectly acceptable for alternatives to handwriting to be explored:

Teachers provide for pupils who need help with communication, language and literacy through:

- *using texts that pupils can read and understand;*
- *using visual and written materials in different formats, including large print, symbol text and Braille;*
- *using ICT, other technological aids and taped materials;*
- *using alternative and augmentative communication, including signs and symbols;*
- *using translators, communicators and amanuenses.*

A standard PC set-up may be loaded with a commercial word processor such as 'Word' (Microsoft) may be quite sufficient to motivate a child who has been deterred from recording using traditional pen and paper. Some children with ASD may benefit from one or more of the adaptations suggested here.

Mice can present problems:

- Relating the movement of the mouse over a table or mat to movement of the arrow on the screen can be a problem. Temple Grandin (2000b) suggests that a paper arrow that looks *exactly* like the arrow on the screen should be taped to the mouse.
- A tracker ball or joystick remains stationary on the desk, and this may prove easier to operate. They can be larger in size giving more room for the hand to control the ball, joystick and buttons. On some, the buttons can be programmed so that a single click can achieve 'select'. In addition the joystick can be programmed for only one movement at a time, either vertical or horizontal (Inclusive Technology).
- 'Little Mouse' and 'Tiny Mouse' (Inclusive Technology), which fit better into the younger or smaller palm, are now available.
- The 'Mouse' settings and the Accessibility options in the 'Control Panel' (Start, Settings) options for Windows are worth investigating. They enable the keypad to be used instead of the mouse, the speed of the mouse to be reduced and the mouse keys to be changed to left-handed orientation.

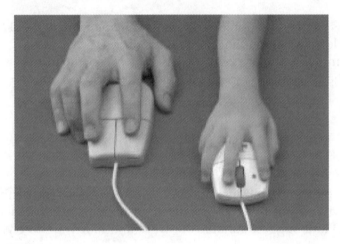

Figure 7.1 Little Mouse and Tiny Mouse

The Standard QWERTY keyboard may be too cluttered, confusing and contain too much information. A range of alternatives exist:

- The National Institute for the Blind, Inclusive Technology, and other agencies, produce lower case letters to stick over the keys. These come in a variety of foreground and background colours.
- A huge range of alternative designs of keyboard can be purchased. Simplified keyboards with less keys, lower case letters or alphabetic layout are available, see for example 'Big Keys' (Inclusive Technology).
- Position the keyboard close to the screen for those pupils who need to simultaneously see the keyboard and the work they are producing on screen.
- Metal key guards fit over the conventional keyboard and can help to prevent fingers slipping and resting on to more than one key.
- The 'Keyboard' in 'Control Panel' (Start, Settings) options for Windows is worth investigating. Auto key repeat can be switched off, which is very convenient for the child whose finger lingers on one key; the repeat rate and repeat delay can also be adjusted. Sticky keys, filter keys and toggle keys in the Accessibility options are also worth investigating.

- Programs to teach basic keyboard familiarity such as 'First Keys To Literacy' (Iota) or even touch-typing programs such as 'Type To Learn' (Sunburst/Tag) and 'Touch Type' ((Iota), along with tuition, will be necessary if the child is to exploit the potential of a computer. It is surprising how many students are issued with new portable word processors as if this was a magic wand for recording. After 'pecking at print' for a while they soon become frustrated and the machine gathers dust on a shelf.

Figure 7.2 Big Keys

Visual Display Units vary considerably:

- Modern VDUs present fewer problems of flicker but it still is worth experimenting with different types and size of screen before purchasing.
- Reflections from artificial light, flicker from fluorescent lights and sunlight from windows can be very uncomfortable and distracting. Position the computer with this in mind.
- Screen guards can reduce reflection and brightness of the screen. In addition the colour can be moderated and for prolonged computer use a guard may be used on health and safety grounds.
- 'Individuals with visual processing problems often find it easier to read if black print is printed on colour paper to reduce contrast. Try light tan, light blue, grey or light green paper. Avoid bright yellow as it may hurt the individual's eyes' (Grandin 2000b). Experiment with different foreground and background colours for the word processor and other programs.

What about standard handwriting practice? There are computer programs that claim to help with handwriting practice. For example, 'Startwrite' (Sherston) produces printouts of standard styles of handwriting. Various levels of dotted line offer more or less help to the child who copies over the text. In addition arrows can be added to show the direction for the pen or pencil to take.

For many children word processing is not being proposed as an alternative to handwriting but as an additional means of recording that may motivate the child. Word processing may become the preferred medium of recording by a child and, particularly for the child with limited learning ability, time may be better spent on mastering keyboard or touch typing skills rather than continuing frustrating and demotivating handwriting practice. This is not a decision to be taken lightly and should involve lengthy consultation with all those concerned, not least the parents and child.

2. Planning and drafting

Although transcription skills have been considered here first, they are really a secondary issue. You have got to have *something* to write to make use of these skills. Planning and drafting may require considerable adult or peer group input, that is, unless writing is to amount to little more than copying from the board, a book, another child or support staff notes. It is important that the helper does not do the entire task for the child. Equally important is that the child is not 'thrown in at the deep end' and left to it. At first offer a heavily structured situation in which the child has only to make limited choices. Early on success is important, especially where a child has experienced many years of failure in the writing task. Later on reduce the prompts and require more of the child.

Fixation on surface details is a danger that haunts the writing process and this is a particular problem for children with ASD who are prone to obsessive behaviours. Brent Robinson (1994) suggests switching off the screen at first, brainstorming ideas, and typing these in 'blind'. Only when a few ideas, perhaps just key words, are recorded, the screen is switched back on. These ideas can then be 'fleshed out'. Spelling, grammar, formatting and so on can be considered later in the process and are covered here in Section 3.

A simple 'writing frame' is a supportive starting point. The form this writing frame takes can vary considerably to suit the individual child. Start with some lists of words, which are identified as 'key' areas in the writing task. These could just as easily be key pictures or symbols or photos as an 'aide-memoire'. For a child who is able and willing to participate in discussion, start together by identifying the main parts of the story or description you wish to record and come back later to 'flesh them out'.

Inspiration and Kidspiration (Inspiration Software Inc.) are planning software that allows a range of diagrammatic formats such as flowcharts, branched hierarchies, idea maps and concept maps that can be converted to text notes and expanded.

Typical on-screen word lists

my cat can jump run eat sleep play	The centurion has a toga a spear a helmet a sword a shield sandals	We got the beaker water salt bunsen stand gauze matches glass mixer We mixed the Etc.
Year 2 Pet Story	**Primary History Lesson**	**Year 9 Science Experiment**

On-screen word grids such as Clicker (Inclusive Technology) is one of a number of programs that can support the use of key words in a grid on screen. The grid works in combination with a word processor. Some word processors such as 'Talking Write Away' (BlackCat) have the facility to run on-screen word grids. Words from the grid can be selected using the mouse and are then placed directly into the word processor. They speed up the writing process by removing some of the spelling and typing tasks, allowing pupils to focus on the creative side of writing. They also act as a framework to remind the pupil of the things that are to be included in the story and even their sequence and order.

Collaborative work is supported and encouraged. The standard keyboard can still be used so that joint work with one or more pupils is possible. The screen is the focus of attention during collaborative work, which can be a useful moderating factor for a child reluctant to make eye to eye contact or hesitant about social interaction. Operation of the grid gives the child a differentiated input into the situation while more able pupils are still able to contribute. Circles of Friends (Newton and Wilson 1998) approaches can be a good way to capitalise on and exploit peer group support both in the collaborative writing exercise and as a way of valuing the computer input of the focus child.

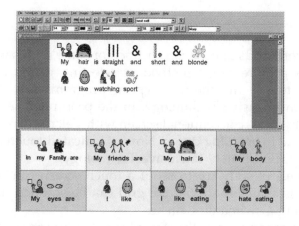

Figure 7.3 Words and symbols

Words may not be enough for some children with ASD. There are children who need additional support to recognise and be motivated to use this writing frame approach to recording.

- Symbols alongside or even instead of the words may be necessary to aid reading and/or understanding. The program 'Writing with Symbols' (Widgit) produces Rebus symbols above words on its own word processor or can produce grids.
- Pictures, usually line drawings or artist's impressions can be generated within most 'on screen' grid programs such as Clicker. A collection of clip art included with the program covers most of the common words, though nouns tend to be easier than verbs.
- Digital photographic images can be fed into most of the grids. You may have to experiment with how best to format the images. These may be from collections of commercially available photographic images, see for example those in Microsoft Clip Art Gallery.
- A digital camera image of the actual object, person etc. may be the only meaningful image for some children with ASD. For example, the very tripod scratches and all, in the surroundings of the lab where they did the experiment, may be the only image for the word 'tripod' that the child can accept and relate to in attempting a written description.

Figure 7.4 Grids help both transcription and composition

Mouse operated word grids may be too abstract for some pupils with ASD. The touch sensitive screen is a more direct method of selecting words or pictures, circumventing the need to use the mouse. Typical programs are 'Touch' and 'Touch Balloons' both from Inclusive Technology. In the past touch sensitive screens were stuck on to the front of the conventional screen with Velcro strips. These tended to be unreliable and prone to breaking down. Now a dedicated touch sensitive screen can be purchased, e.g. 'MicroTouch' (Inclusive Technology).

Look in the details of software to see if a touch screen can operate it. A switch version of Clicker is available so that the grid can be scanned in various ways and words selected using a switch or switches.

The concept keyboards, such as those produced by 'Informax' (Granada Learning), provide a larger and more concrete way for children to select the main items involved in a story or description.

- The keyboard is usually an A3 size pad onto which a paper overlay fits.
- As with the on-screen grids, the number and size of cells on the overlay can be varied to suit the ability of the child.
- Many permutations of words, symbols, pictures, photos can be placed on the overlay.
- In older non-verbal children and adults, touch is often their most reliable sense (Grandin 2000). Tactile letters, shapes, symbols, etc. can be cut and pasted onto the overlay.
- Each overlay is accompanied by a program, which must be loaded. In addition a word processor must be loaded and running.
- When a cell on the pad is pressed, single letters, words, phrases or whole sentences are place on the word processor on screen.

Intellikeys (Inclusive Technology) have produced an easier version of the concept keyboard in that the overlays carry a bar code. When a new overlay is placed on the pad it automatically gives the computer the information it needs, saving the loading of software and allowing the pad to be used immediately with virtually any modern word processor. The additional program Overlay Maker allows you to make your own overlays relevant to pupil needs.

Commercially produced overlays and grids or custom made?

There are now a vast range of commercially available overlays and grids. In some cases these match up to areas within the National Curriculum. In addition many of these are freely available once you have bought the original program. Readers would be well advised to visit the Intellikeys site (Inclusive Technology) and also the Clicker site (http://www.cricksoft.com) where hundreds of examples are available. Many users never produce their own overlays or grids but are happy to use those readily available 'off the shelf'. There are a number of advantages in this:

- the standard of production is usually very high;
- the novice user may not feel competent to program their own overlay or grid;
- ready made overlays save valuable teacher time.

Custom made grids and overlays are those made by the teacher, support assistant, parent etc. using words, pictures and photos that relate to and reflect the interest and needs of a particular child or group. They come into their own for the child who is reluctant or anxious about the recording task.

- By reflecting the personal interests of the child they provide motivation and confidence to begin the recording task.
- They offer a more concrete representation of reality; for example photos of hobbies, pastimes, places of interest can be pasted onto the concept keyboard overlay, or digital images loaded into a Clicker grid.
- 'Many autistic children get fixated on one subject such as trains or maps. The best way to deal with fixations is to use them to motivate school work' (Grandin 2000a), for example by images on a grid or overlay.
- The process of making the overlay or grid provides an opportunity for creativity, imagination and planning. Even the non-speaking child may be involved in choosing appropriate photos, sequencing and ordering them for sticking on to an overlay.
- Useful language and social opportunities arise from both the process of making and using overlays or grids.

Are ideas linear? A small number of children may find it hard to relate the jumble of ideas inside their head to a written record on paper. Even modern word processors, with their ability to cut, move and paste items around, still end up with a linear representation of ideas from left to right on the page.

Desktop publishing or art programs offer the ability to place objects and words randomly on the page and then move them around at will. Early on the child will need help and support in choosing and recording words and pictures, or even drawing the pictures for him/herself. The child in a 'brainstorming' exercise can do their arrangement on the screen. Children with ASD often like art programs and allowing them to experiment can be a good way of motivating them and moving towards adding words and pictures that relate to classroom based activities. An example is shown in Figure 7.5, where pictures have been randomly placed on the page. Later the child could drag and drop them into an order that had meaning for them, and perhaps also 'drag and drop' words or phrases to match. Using the paint tools the child can colour or alter the images. Again there is useful language work to be gained from discussion of this activity with an adult and/or another child or children with the focus of attention being the screen rather than eye-to-eye contact.

'My World' (Inclusive Technology) is a program based upon this principle of 'dragging and dropping' a combination of pictures and words onto a screen. The user can add his/her own text and drag and drop this onto the screen. Hundreds of ready-made screens are available most of which relate to early learning or primary curriculum activities.

Figure 7.5 Typical My World screen, e.g. dinosaur, e.g. volcano etc.

3. Revising and editing

The advantages of a word processor come into their own here. Work done on a word processor is often said to be 'provisional' as it can very easily be corrected, altered and updated. Unlike traditional pen and paperwork, mistakes or decisions to change the layout of the work are not penalised by tedious and time consuming re-writing or re-typing. See example of Dermot's handwritten and word processed work in Chapter 5 (Figure 5.13).

The sheer number and complexity of some of the powerful features of word processing mean that for many of us we neither know nor use half the features that are at our fingertips. Even so, for those pupils with poor handwriting, poor artistic abilities, or who are weak at spelling and grammar, even a limited knowledge of word processing can enable them to produce elegant finished work that is as good as or better than that of many of their peers. For the child with ASD this stage in the writing process needs to be handled with care.

- A child with ASD may be prone to concentration on minor details and trivia and obsessed with details. The multifaceted features of editing and revising themselves could all too easily become an unhealthy focus of attention.
- Some children have a tendency to delete any work that is not 'perfect'. Save work regularly, set auto save to a short period, click on the 'save' icon regularly, or use the keyboard short cut (CTRL + 'S'). Then even when work is deleted on screen you can go back, print out the work and celebrate with the child what has been achieved.
- Regular printouts are important as tangible evidence of the good quality work being produced. Children are often keen to show these to parents, teachers and fellow students.
- Avoid competitive comparison with other pupils' work but rather have two or three examples of 'good enough' practice. Set a small number of achievable parameters within which editing and revising is to occur, standard rules for font size and type, where to underline and use bold, etc.
- The 'control hypothesis' suggests that being able to exert control over a situation is very motivating. The tools of editing and revising by giving power over the writing process can be used to motivate recording.
- The basic elements of word processing can be picked up by observations of others. Many children with ASD surprise their parents by learning word processing and other computer programs by observing brothers, sisters and friends. However, the more powerful features of WP, such as multi-tasking, may need to be taught or modelled for the child.

The size of font

Type of font, , comic sans MS, *Blackadder ITC*, **jokerman**, *Lucida handwriting etc.*

Colour of foreground and background

<u>Underline</u>, | Borders |, outline, EMBOSS

SMALL CAPS

 cut  copy paste

 Insert pictures or symbols tables and graphs

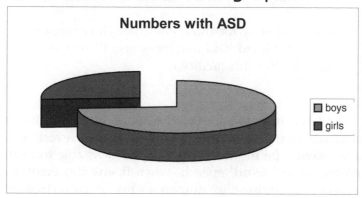

Numbers with ASD

boys
girls

- Use
- bullet points
2. Use
3. numbers

Figure 7.6 Provisional qualities of word processing

A talking word processor, such as Talking Write Away, is often useful for Granada Learning pupils with ASD for one or more of the following reasons:

- it provides feedback so that the child can more easily detect spelling and typing errors themselves;
- it provides feedback so that the child can more easily and in a non-judgemental way become aware of errors or inconsistencies in meaning;
- it can provide a less threatening focus of attention where paired or group work is taking place.

Headphones can be useful for individual work:

- they cut out intrusion and interruption in an active and busy classroom situation for pupils who are prone to distraction;
- some children with ASD like the security and seclusion of headphone use;
- in a quiet lesson headphones avoid interruption to the rest of the class.

Spellcheckers are included with most word processors.

- They offer a non-judgemental way to alert the child to spelling and typing errors.
- Hand held spellcheckers, such as those produced by Franklin (available from iANSYST), represent very good value as they have a massive spelling vocabulary and offer 'phonic' as well as word matching facilities, so for example typing in the word 'sycologist' would still result in some 'ps' words being offered such as 'psychologist'.
- Spellcheckers offer a mechanical means to deal with spelling which may motivate and capture the attention of the child with ASD. Yet such devices can lead to an increased awareness of poor spelling and greater motivation to find the correct spelling for words.
- A 'talking spellchecker' may be necessary for those children who cannot read the word lists offered. (Both Franklin for hand held machines and Write Outloud and TextHelp for computer based WP offer this facility.)

Auto correction facilities allow the user to instruct the word processor to automatically correct common errors (see for example, 'Tools', 'Auto Correct' in MS Word). For example, I would often type the word 'speach' but was able to instruct auto correct to always type the correct word 'speech' when it saw this error. Such mechanical forms of correction, in contrast to human forms of correction, may fascinate and capture the imagination of the child with ASD. As with spellcheckers this may offer a less threatening and more acceptable way to focus on common errors.

Predictive word processors, such as Penfriend, Co-Writer and Predictability, consider the first two or three letters typed in by the user and then offer an on-screen word list of probable completed words. 'Psy' for example would probably offer a list containing 'psychologist', 'psychologies', 'psychology'. The user would then select the correct word.

Speech recognition is one of the most recent types of word processing available. In theory the child (or adult) speaks into a microphone and the words appear on the page of a word processor. Dragon software has been quoted here because, at present, this appears to be better suited to children's voices (http://www.dragonsys.com).

- Two types of system exist. 'Discrete' requires a stilted form of speech, each word being delivered slowly and clearly; however, some children still prefer it. Dragon 'Classic' is an example of this type. 'Continuous speech', on the other hand, allows entry of words in normal speech. Go for the most recent software for this type of system, Dragon 'Naturally Speaking' (http://www.lhsl.com/naturallyspeaking), which is cheap and probably as good as many others.
- The most up-to-date processor and plenty of on board memory is essential.
- For laptops check that the appropriate sound card is fitted.
- Long enrolment for the computer to learn the child's speech patterns is not needed with recent editions. However do not underestimate the amount of time needed for the child to become familiar with the software and hardware.
- 1:1 support both technical and for learning is essential in the early stages and this can only be slowly withdrawn and on a trial basis once the child is assured of success.
- The error rate is still quite high even for experienced users. Patience, determination and a willingness to use the various correction procedures are essential. This is not for the child who easily becomes frustrated.
- Getting the thing to work in a totally silent and undisturbed room is one thing, the hurly burly of a mainstream classroom is quite another. Timetabling and management of the voice recognition system is key to its success.

All this having been said, the computer based and mechanical nature of the medium may be the motivator that induces your child to an interest in speech, that has otherwise eluded you. One of the case studies in Chapter 5 (Derick) gives an interesting insight into the early use of voice recognition with a pupil with ASD.

iANSYST (Software Appendix) can give up-to-date advice regarding latest voice recognition technology and accessories such as microphones, sound cards etc.

If you want to learn more from the practical experience of others why not visit the BECTa web site and search for speech recognition (http://www.becta.org.uk/).

The research by BECTa relating to Literacy indicated interesting findings that may offer potential for some children with ASD:

☐ There was a clear improvement in users' speech. It was slower and more distinct
☐ By the end of each session there was a noticeable improvement in articulation and voice projection
☐ Because the students needed to develop dictation skills, they became more able to bullet point and draft out ideas quickly
☐ The speech recognition software positively encourages punctuation
☐ The on-screen correction box encourages correct word recognition
☐ There is complete freedom to use extended vocabulary
☐ The systems help with thinking ideas through
☐ Having control of the PC gives time to structure thoughts

---

8 The Internet

The web, for both teachers and students, can be an exciting and useful tool or can be a very frustrating and angry experience. Easy guides on how to use the Internet are available from, for example one of BECTa's information sheets (http://www.becta.org.uk).

Our advice is to start by going to known sites that you have been advised of. In this case you will have an address which you have seen in a book or magazine, or a friend has given to you. Here is one example: http://www.nas.org.uk (National Autistic Society). You type this into the window at the top of your Internet screen (delete or overtype the one that is there). Then just hit the Return (Enter) key.

Follow 'hot links' to other sites that look interesting. Anything you see on a site which is underlined and causes your cursor to change to a 'hand' is probably a 'hot link'.

- If you start to get lost remember you can use the back arrow at the top of the screen to retrace your steps. Or use the 'Home' button to return to your starting point.
- If you fail to find what you want with the above steps you may then want to do a search. Why not start by searching sites that you know may contain information about autism, rather than searching the whole of the Internet.
- It is well worth reading a simple guide to searching to avoid a frustrating exercise. Again BECTa offer a simple information sheet at http://www.becta.org.uk.

Website starting points

'Seek and ye shall find' but . . .

- don't try surfing the whole web first time;
- use the following sites as starting points;
- they have information relating to autism;
- they have hundreds of links to other sites;
- sites do change over time so do not be put off if some of these do not work.

Figure 8.1 Web starting points

National associations

The National Autistic Society (NAS), http://www.nas.org.uk

This is a natural starting point for the UK. Like many sites it has a good explanation of what autism and Asperger's syndrome are. The home page is simply laid out with a comprehensive range of links to other sites and resources.

This is a particularly good site for support for parents, carers and children, which is not surprising as this was the main purpose for the formation of the association back in 1962. Interaction is encouraged with e-mail links, chat rooms and conventional postal links. You can find your own local branch from one of the hot links on the site, http://www.oneworld.org/autism_uk/nas/network.html#list.

Centre for Studies of Autism, http://www.autism.org

Located in Oregon, USA and linked to the Autism Research Institute, one gets the impression that this is a more research based than support based site. This said, there are many useful and informative items here and links to other helpful sites. It starts with a clear and easy to use table of contents, each item being a 'hot link' that takes you to another part of the site. These are sorted into categories, an overview of autism, subgroups and related disorders, issues, interventions, Temple Grandin, Sibling Centre, interviews and other information. The final item is other autism related resources on the Internet, which has a further vast range of links to more sites.

A postal address but no e-mail link is offered.

Advocacy, networking and support

Autism Europe, http://www.autismeurope.arc.be and World Autism Organisation, http://worldautism.org

Both of these sites hope to advance the rights of people with autism and their families. They are typical of sites that have a more political or advocacy role. Both sites start by inviting the user to choose which language they want to operate in. World Autism usefully has a searchable world map to link you to organisations world wide.

Autism Connect, http://www.autism99.org

Claims to be a new, free, non-commercial website that aims to be the first port of call for anyone interested in autism, providing news, events, world maps, and rapid access to other websites with information on autism.

Autism Connect aims to be a worldwide, interactive, personalised forum for the sharing of information by people whose lives are touched by autism. This includes people with autism, their parents, friends, educators and therapists, as well as researchers.

Dimensions Speech, Language, and Learning Services North, http://www.dimensionsspeech.com

A site that concentrates on computer-based therapy for individuals with autism. It has some good links and articles also.

D. Murray and Mike Lesser's site, www.shifth.mistral.co.uk/autism

On autism and computing, with short video clips to illustrate the different issues such as self-esteem, turn taking, communication and sociability.

The AZ Method, www.cypnet.com

How one family used video footage to develop language skills in their child with ASD.

The Geneva Centre for Autism, www.autism.net

A leading source of training for individuals with ASD and their communities.

On-line magazines

Autism Today, http://www.autismtoday.com

This is an example of an on-line magazine with articles, artwork, book reviews, items submitted by users, news of conferences and so on.

Software and hardware

Xplanatory, http://www.canterbury.ac.uk/xplanatory/supply/supply.htm

This is an alphabetic listing of both software and hardware suppliers and special educational needs suppliers, based in the UK. Contact details are given for each company. These pages are part of a much larger site run by Mike Blamires which has a wealth of information on special educational needs: http://www.canterbury.ac.uk/xplanatory.

British Educational Software Database, http://besd.becta.org.uk

This is part of the BECTa site. Although a general educational database it can be searched for specific items. You may like to try a search for 'Autism' as with many sites you will find little specifically on this area but there are some useful programs under the general heading of 'Language and Communication Difficulties'.

Inclusive Technology, http://www.inclusive.co.uk

Follow the links on the home page for the on-line catalogues of software and hardware for special educational needs. Inclusive Technology has one of the most comprehensive ranges of software. This site also has some very informative articles, 'What is Autism' http://www.inclusive.co.uk/support/autism.shtml, and 'Autism and ICT', http://www.inclusive.co.uk/infosite/autism.shtml.

SEMERC (Granada), http://www.granadalearning.co.uk/school
(follow the links to the SEMERC section)

They have similar products to Inclusive Technology, see for example 'Switch On Travel', and the My World series.

Autism specific software sites

There is not much ASD specific software around but here are some sites to try.

Gaining Face, http://www.ccoder.com/GainingFace

Software that helps people with Asperger's syndrome, high-functioning autism and similar issues learn to recognise facial expressions.

My Friend Ben, http://www.asilesp.com

Funded by the European Union, it is a multimedia CD-ROM for young adults with Asperger's syndrome.

Dimensions Speech, Language, and Learning Services North, http://www.dimensionsspeech.com

This site has already been quoted above, but if you follow the links on the page to 'articles' you should find references for software relevant to speech and language therapy.

Education

The National Curriculum Online, http://www.nc.uk.net/home.html

Contains all of the revised programmes of study. For those pupils who are currently performing significantly below the National Curriculum levels, or are 'working towards' level one, the 'P' scales may offer a more motivating means of monitoring achievement.

The 'P' scales, and the associated curriculum materials, http://www.nc.uk.net/ld/

Along with the level descriptors have created nine pre-National Curriculum levels and have broken down further the existing levels 1 and 2. All children are now on one of these levels. Level 1 only involves an 'encounter', i.e. being present when a lesson is going on.

British Educational Communications and Technology agency (BECTa), http://www.becta.org.uk/start/index.html

This is a good general education site. The home page is well laid out; this reference takes you to the 'Where do I start' section of the site. Although not specific to autism there is useful guidance on how to use ICT to aid access to literacy, numeracy and other areas of the National Curriculum, how to make best use of computers in the classroom, and how to make use of ICT for pupils with special educational needs. Amongst other things there is advice on safe use of the Internet for children, (http://www.becta.org.uk/technology/safetyseminar/holder.html). The BECTa Advice and Information Centre contains amongst other things a range of useful information sheets; three have already been quoted here.

New Opportunities Fund, http://www.nof.org.uk/edu/ict/main.cfm

Teachers and librarians can find out about the subsidised training that is available for them. On the home page search the 'Provider Database' to see what local INSET providers there are. Disappointingly there is no option available to search for either

Language and Communication or Autism; the closest match is 'Severe and Complex SEN', for which you will find seven providers in the Southeast of England.

School subjects

Searching may well find sites specifically relating to school subjects, particularly. Here are just two examples as a 'taster' but there are many more if you search.

Maths Forum, http://mathforum.com

This site covers a range of common maths applications; try for example the pages on 'What is a Tessellation?', http://forum.swarthmore.edu/sum95/suzanne/whattess.html.

Jen's Crucible Web Page, http://www.geocities.com/CollegePark/Classroom/3085/crucible.html

Most of the set readers for exams have information posted on the net. This page has sections for teachers, sections for pupils, notes on main characters, advice for essay writing etc.

Enthusiasms, fixations, obsessions

Thomas the Tank Engine, Pokemon, etc., http://www.thomasthetankengine.com/home/homepage.html

This is typical of the type of pupil interest site that you can access once you become familiar with word searches. This site combines movement, sound and colour and it is interactive and has games, for example, guess which engine is in the engine shed. Children with autism often have a fascination with trains, transport and wheeled vehicles. But the obsession can be anything: string, light switches, you name it, but you will probably find something on the web. Start from the child's obsession and use the computer to draw the child into a wider world.

Temple Grandin (2000a) suggests,

Many autistic children get fixated on one subject such as trains or maps. The best way to deal with fixations is to use them to motivate school work. If the child likes trains, then use trains to teach reading and math. Read a book about a train and do math problems with trains. For example, calculate how long it takes for a train to go between New York and Washington.

Sites run by people with ASD

http://www.geocities.com/HotSprings/Resort/3613/

This is Richard Hudson's home page; he has Asperger's syndrome. It is an example of a site managed by a person with ASD and, as Richard points out, many sites give you the clinical definition of autism but 'to really answer the question what is autism it should be asked to people who actually have autism and live with it everyday. . .' It has some good links if you want to hear more (Jane Healy).

9 Buying and using your own computer

The intention here is to give you some simple tips to follow in buying your own computer and getting started with it. Clearly we cannot give detailed technical advice about specific systems. What we will try to do is consider some of the software and hardware described in this book and suggest some considerations in purchasing computer equipment and getting started with it in your own home. In some cases we have referred to the five qualities of ICT outlined in Chapter 4 and, depending on which are most relevant to your child, have suggested which elements of a sales package to concentrate on.

1. General considerations

- Know what you want the computer to do. Hopefully the chapters in this book have helped you define much more clearly the profile of ASD that applies to your child and also some ICT solutions that may be worth trying. Will you need to add specialist hardware such as switches or a concept keyboard? Will you want to load additional software? Write a list of the things you want as an aid in seeking the best buy from shops or companies.

- The standard computer set-up shown in Figure 6.2 is worth reviewing and, if you feel that you may need some of the adaptations suggested there, then again list these.

- Don't buy a computer just for a child with autism. This may sound like strange advice after the enthusiasm we have shown in this book. But bear in mind the social qualities of a computer that have been outlined, the countless opportunities and motivations for social activity as a result of children and adults using a computer together. Remember also that many children and adults with ASD learnt how to use a computer by watching other people using one. Especially if you do not already own a computer, do not go out and buy one just for the child with autism.

- Buy a good family computer, unless there are very good reasons to do otherwise. Make sure that it has utility software such as a word processor and games so that all members of the family will enjoy using it. Most of the specialist software and hardware mentioned in this book can easily be added. In the unfortunate, and unlikely event, that the child with ASD does not like the computer you will not have wasted your money as other members of the family will have use of it. In addition as long as no pressure is put on them he/she may well come back to the computer at a later date.

- Guarantee and customer support are important unless you or a close friend are a computer buff. Do you feel confident to set up the computer? Would you be happy to follow telephone helpline instructions if things go wrong? If not it may well be worth paying extra for support on-site, especially if you have a child who is prone to experiment with software and hardware.

- Positioning, in other words where you will put the computer in your home, is an important issue. It needs to be safe but easy access is important for regular use.

- Insurance may be included in your home contents cover but check that an expensive system does not have to be specifically listed.
- Training for you, the child and anyone else who will use the machine may be necessary. Tutorials on screen are included with most software. Parents' centres, local authorities and support groups may offer training sessions. Informal help and guidance from workmates and friends is still the most common form of training.

2. Specific points to look for in a computer

- Processor speed is usually shown as Megahertz (MHz). The bigger the number, the faster the machine. This is probably not an important issue where word processing is your main aim (provisional qualities from Chapter 4). Faster machines may help you where multimedia programs, virtual reality games, simulations and so on are important (quality of interactivity, Chapter 4).
- Memory is usually shown as Mbs of RAM and 64 Mb is the minimum you should look for, but get as much as you can. Together processor speed and amount of RAM may affect speed of starting programs and possibly 'surfing' the net. This may be a consideration for children with short concentration spans or where the qualities of 'capacity and range' are important for your child (Chapter 4).
- Hard drives are measured in gigabytes (Gb) and 5 Gb or more is now common for a desktop machine. Again, if you intend to store a large number of multimedia programs, invest in large hard drives.
- Upgrading processor, memory, etc., later is possible with most machines, but most of us never go to the trouble or expense. It is easier and cheaper to get what you need when you first buy the machine.
- Monitors are quite useable in 15 inch size. Larger sizes cost more money but a 17 or 21 inch may be more comfortable to use and better suited if you want to encourage collaborative use of the computer by more than one person. The screen type may be a critical factor for some children with ASD and it may be worth trying different ones, including laptops, to see which one they are most comfortable with. Remember also that screen settings, background and foreground colour, contrast, brightness, size and so on, can be customised on most operating systems (in Windows through START, Control Panel and then using the Accessibility options or Screen options).
- Mice and keyboards alternatives are discussed in Chapter 6 if the child has problems with the standard set-up.
- Modem is the device that connects the computer to the phone line so that you can use the Internet and e-mail. You will also need some software loaded to run with the modem. Modem speed is measured in kilo bauds per second (Kbps); get the fastest you can afford. 56.6 kbps is currently the norm. Problems establishing Internet access and setting up an e-mail account are common and if you do not feel confident again it is worth buying from a company who include on-site help with this. Where the ICT qualities of 'capacity and range' (Chapter 4) are important for your child then pay particular attention to a fast, reliable connection.
- A printer may be included in the package you buy. When buying a printer you need to decide whether or not you want colour. If good quality text and speed is more important, go for a laser printer. As well as the cost and quality of the printer, it is well worth asking the price of replacement inks as this can come as a nasty shock some time later. The monitor and a printer may be key considerations where the qualities of 'automaticity' and 'provisionality' are significant for your child (see Chapter 4).
- Multimedia features to check out are the speed of the CD drive, the sound card and speakers, video card and monitor. Most computers have these now but their importance is greater in the case of a child who is mainly exploiting the qualities of 'interactivity' and 'capacity and range' (Chapter 4).

- Camera and scanner and other devices may be included in a sales package. But they are often bottom of the range and if these are important features for your child, it may be worth buying a cheaper computer and investing your money in a better quality camera, etc.

3. Software issues

The software on your machine is probably more important in determining its successful and regular use in the home than considerations of modem, RAM, cache and all of the other paraphernalia that is prominent in PC sales and advertising.

- When buying your own machine beware special offers of massive packages of software. Do you want or need all of these items? Does it contain programs that directly relate to your child's interests and the school curriculum?
- The most used item in any package is the word processor; make sure that it is compatible with the word processor used in your child's school.
- 'Word' (MS Office) is the most common word processor (in English schools) and may well be the one your child has seen and used in school, or college or on work experience.
- Loading your own software is easy. It is surprising how many people baulk at this task without even reading the 'Installation/Set-up' instructions. There are usually only two or three steps to follow, well documented, and then the disc will automatically load with a few simple to follow instructions on screen.
- Wherever possible, trial software. An LEA ICT centre may allow you to do this or the company may offer demonstration discs.
- Networks in schools or companies are a problem. Teachers need to get permission from the Network Manager (usually the ICT coordinator in schools) to load new software and may need to ask them to do it for them.
- Software of use to a range of pupils may be worth a school purchasing a site licence for and loading on to the whole network. More specialist software for one or two pupils with autism may be better loaded on to one machine, but choose a machine that you have regular and easy access to.
- Licences for software vary:
  - a single user licence is the cheapest but you can only load the software on to one machine, e.g. your home machine;
  - a site licence is more expensive but good value when you want to load the software on to a large number of machines and laptops that are used by school staff and pupils;
  - a compromise in terms of price is a user licence to load onto a limited number of machines, e.g. five.

4. School issues

- Is there a particular teacher, ICT coordinator, tutor, class teacher who could advise you on applications most relevant to your child?
- Is there a teacher who could spare a few minutes every so often to give you ongoing help and advice?
- Are there encyclopaedias, CDs, SATs primers etc. that directly relate to the school curriculum? If so, try to do a deal to get these included in your initial package.
- Are there Internet sites that directly relate to exams, subjects and interests from school? (Some are suggested in Chapter 8.)
- Are there formal or informal e-mail support networks for schoolwork and interests amongst your child's friends?

Will you be word processing a lot of your school assignments and other work? Will you be using spreadsheets and other applications? If so, check out that your home machine comes with software compatible to what you are used to in school.

5. Desktop versus laptop issues

The question of whether to buy a laptop computer sometimes arises where the child needs to use the machine in school and especially at secondary school where they need to go from room to room for each lesson. Some practical issues need to be considered.

- Durability. Cheap dedicated word processors such as the Star Writer or Dreamwriter can take a few knocks. More expensive portable PCs are fragile.
- Weight. Is your child an Olympic weightlifter, able to carry PC, leads, power supply etc. along with books, PE kit, lunch box and a violin every Tuesday?
- Security. Who will pay for insurance? Is there secure storage in school? Is there a back-up computer in event of loss or breakage, important for students dependent on a machine for GCSE and other exams? Is machine security marked?
- Bullying. Will the responsibility of carrying an expensive computer around school and to and from school be an additional worry for the child?
- What happens when it goes wrong? Is there a maintenance agreement? Who will sort out day-to-day difficulties?
- Printing. Do you have a printer at home, is there a base in school to print off work or is the child additionally going to carry a printer round?
- Training. For child, staff and parents, this needs to be considered. Will the child need keyboard or touch typing to exploit word processing potential?
- School staff. They need to be informed of the purposes of a portable and be willing to accept word processed work.
- Laptop screens. Can present problems for people with visual difficulties but are preferred by some children and adults with ASD.

6. Adding switches, keyboards and other hardware

There is not room here to describe every additional device but most, such as switches, concept keyboards and touch sensitive screens, come with simple-to-follow instructions. If you do not feel confident to have a go yourself, you need to establish some 'lines of support', to help set up and maintain additional devices.

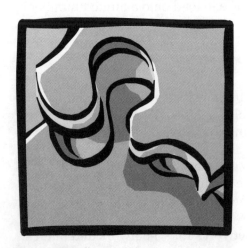

**I'm no good at technical things!
Yes but can you do jigsaws?**

Figure 9.1 Jigsaw

It is surprising the number of people who happily embark on daunting and intricate 2000 piece jigsaws yet baulk at the idea of working out how to put together six to eight crudely shaped interfaces and leads to assemble a computer.

The basic rules for assembling computer parts are similar to jigsaws:

- Look for clues in the shape and size of sockets and leads. Most leads, printer, RS232, etc. are shaped so that they can only fit in one place.
- Never force a part, ease it in, and if it feels wrong, as though it won't fit, don't force it.
- Look for clues: on the back of your computer there are often symbols or pictures above the slots to tell you what has to go in there.
- Read the instructions.

Locating the RS232 port (serial port) is key to success for attaching a number of additional devices, switches, concept keyboards and so on. It may be known as the Communications port or the RS232. There may be more than one Com 1 and Com 2 and whichever you plug the switch into you are bound to choose the wrong one!

Switches often have a lead with a jack plug on it. This does not push directly into the serial port but into a small box which has jack plug sockets on one side and a lead to the serial port on the other.

Figure 9.2 Serial port

Hardware such as switches and concept keyboards may well have software that has to be loaded to run it.

When you have installed new hardware and software you may well have to shut down your machine and start it up again before it will work. If things go wrong, shutting down and starting again is often the first thing to try.

Computer Buying Checklist

Name of Shop/Company _____ Computer Name _____

(Compare at least three systems before choosing)

1. Processor: probably Pentium with speed in Mhz: 200, 300, 400, . . .?

2. RAM (Memory): at least 64 Mb but get more if you can afford it.

3. Cache: we have not mentioned this but get at least 256 kb.

4. Case: tower, desktop or mini-tower (think about positioning issues).

5. Hard Drive – get at least 2 Gb but again get as much as you can for your money.

6. Are multimedia features included?

7. Monitor: size 15, 17, 19, 21 inch?

8. What printer, inkjet (bubble jet) or laser? How much do replacement inks cost?

9. Modem: at least 33.6 kbps. 56.6 kbps or more is better.

10. What support is there, in setting up and initial use including Internet and e-mail?

11. What support is there when things go wrong? On-site or return to maker?

12. What training is available for you and your child?

13. What software is included? Is it compatible with your school's software?

14. Will the computer be included in your home contents insurance?

15. Total cost.

© 2002 Colin Hardy, Jan Ogden, Julie Newman and Sally Cooper. *Autism and ICT*. Published by David Fulton Publishers. ISBN 1-85436-824-X.

10 Conclusions

We began this book with the comments of a number of teachers and parents about children they knew or taught who had ASD and we will end in this fashion.

On a recent visit to a school, one of the authors mentioned that the computer program 'IEP Writer' (Learn How Publications) was a helpful way to structure staff discussion of suitable targets and strategies for a pupil's individual education plan (IEP). In passing he added, 'oh, and it's a good way to get the pupil involved, let them sit with you and read the targets and choose some for themselves'. The advice was given with no particular 'category' of pupils in mind, least of all those with ASD. So imagine our surprise when the SENCO ran up to us at the next visit and excitedly told us the following:

> *Charlie (a pupil with autism) has never spoken to me so much, well he still won't look me in the face, but he talks to me looking sideways at the screen. He could not resist the drop-down menu of behaviour targets, reading them out, and choosing those that he felt related to him. I have never got him to discuss his behaviour problems like this before. And it was similar with the strategies. We worked for over an hour and he did not want to go at the end of the session. I urged him to set the success criteria to achievement of the targets on seven or eight out of ten occasions, but he insisted on ten out of ten success. He has been running up to me all week and reporting his progress on the targets.* (SENCO at a large boys' Technology College)

We tell this story because it typifies a problem we have experienced throughout the course of writing this book. Whenever we think we have finished, someone runs up to us and tells us some other interesting tale of ICT use with a child with autism. Similarly with software and hardware, despite noble efforts to adhere to the TTA advice to 'future proof', new items appear on the horizon. In relation to autism we would mention a small number of avenues that readers may like to follow up, depending upon the specific needs and interest of individual children.

The example quoted here of target-setting with a child typifies a commitment throughout the book to pupil involvement. ICT approaches that enhance and facilitate this are very much the order of the day with the prominence of pupil participation in the new draft Code of Practice on Special Educational Needs (DfES 2001).

Mike Blamires in his book *Enabling Technology for Inclusion* (1999, p. 180) points to virtual reality which he suggests, 'like speech recognition . . . until recently had seemed to be within the realms of science fiction'. We have very briefly touched on this in Microworlds in Chapter 6. In Chapter 7 we have cautiously discussed voice recognition and given some references for those who wish to follow it up.

Computer based therapies are another area which has briefly been alluded to, see in particular an article by Valerie Herskowitz (2000) on the Dimensions Speech, Language, and Learning Services North site (Chapter 8). Valerie ponders on what the new millennium may hold. 'Will our clients and students interface with a computer screen rather than a live person? Will we be replaced by a virtual reality speech-language pathologist?'

We hope that, in Chapter 8, we have whetted your appetite for the potential of the Internet, and have given you some suggestions for sites worth further investigation. Sites for advice, support, keeping abreast of the latest research in autism and ICT, and not least for interaction, multiply in number and type each month, giving you and your children the opportunity to share experiences with others.

It is difficult to know where and when to stop but we hope that this book has given you and the children that you work with some ideas of things to try and some avenues worth exploring.

Appendix 1: Software and hardware references

ACE Centre
92 Windmill Road
Wayneflete Road
Headington
Oxford
OX3 7DR
Tel: 01865 763508/759800

Blackcat Educational Software
The Barn
Cwm Camlais
Brecon
Powys
LD3 8LD
Tel: 01874 636835
Fax: 01874 636858

Crick Computing
123 The Drive
Northampton
NN1 2SW

Granada Learning
The Chiswick Centre
414 Chiswick High Road
London
W4 5TF
Tel: 020 8996 3333
Fax: 020 8742 8390
http://www.granadalearning.com/
info@granada-learning.com

iANSYST
The White House
72 Fen Road
Cambridge
CB4 1UN
Freephone: 0500 141515
www.dyslexic.com

Inclusive Technology Ltd
Gateshead Business Park
Delph New Road
Delph
Oldham
OL3 5BX
Tel: 01457 819790
Fax: 01457 819799
http://www.inclusive.co.uk/catalog/home.shtml

Iota Software
Iota House
Wellington Court
Cambridge
CB1 1HZ
Tel: 01223 566788
www.iota.co.uk

Keytools
PO Box 700
Southampton
SO17 1LQ
Tel: 023 8058 4314
Fax: 023 8055 6902
e-mail: info@keytools.com
web: www.keytools.com

Learn How Publications
10 Townsend Avenue
Southgate
London
N14 7HJ
Tel: 020 8886 2262/020 8524 4642
http://www.learnhowpublications.co.uk

Liberator
Whitegates
Swinstead
NG33 4PA
Tel: 01476 550391
Fax: 01476 550357
http://www.liberator.co.uk/lowres/index.htm

REM
Great Western House
Langport
Somerset
TA10 9YU

SherstonSoftware Ltd
Angel House
Sherston
Malmesbury
Wiltshire
SN16 0LH
Tel: 01666 843200
www.sherston.com

Swan Barton
Sherston
Malmesbury
Wiltshire
SN16 0LL
Tel: 01666 840433

TAG
25 Pelham Road
Gravesend
Kent
DA11 0HU
Tel: 01474 537886
www.taglearning.com

Topologika Software
Waterside House
Falmouth Road
Penryn
Cornwall
TR10 8BE
Tel: 01326 377771
http://www.topologika.co.uk

Virtual Reality Systems
Unit 8
Farm Business Centre
East Tytherly Road
Lockerley
Romsey
Hampshire
SO51 0LW

Widgit Software
102 Radford Road
Luton
LU1 1TR

Xemplar Education
700 Great Cambridge Road
Enfield
EN1 3BR

References

Aarons, M. and Gittens, T. (1992) *Autism: a Guide for Parents and Professionals.* London: Routledge.

Anderson, Genan T. (2000) 'Computers in a developmentally appropriate curriculum', *Young Children*, March.

Attwood, T. (1998) *Asperger's Syndrome: a Guide for Parents and Professionals.* London: Jessica Kingsley Publishers.

Baron-Cohen, S. (1996) *Mindblindness: an Essay on Autism and Theory of Mind.* The Massachusetts Institute of Technology Press.

Baron-Cohen, S. (1997) *Autism The Facts.* Oxford: Oxford University Press.

Blamires, M. (1999) *Enabling Technology for Inclusion.* London: Paul Chapman Publishing.

British Educational Communications and Technology Agency, (BECTa), http://www.becta.org.uk/start/index.html accessed 21/08/2001.

Cumine, V., Leach, J. and Stevenson, G. (2000) *Autism in the Early Years,* London: David Fulton Publishers.

Detheridge, T. (1997) 'Bridging the communication gap (for pupils with profound and multiple learning difficulties)', *British Journal of Special Education,* **24** (1).

DfES (2001) new draft *Code of Practice on Special Educational Needs* (July 2001).

Edelson, S. M., PhD *Overview of Autism,* Center for the Study of Autism, Salem, Oregon, http://www.autism.org/overview.html, accessed 27/12/00.

Frith, U. (1989) *Autism: Explaining the Enigma.* Oxford: Blackwell.

Grandin, T. (1995) *Thinking in Pictures,* New York: Vintage Books.

Grandin, T. (2000a) Teaching Tips for Children and Adults with Autism, Centre for Studies of Autism (revised: June 2000), http://www.autism.org/temple/inside.html, accessed 27/12/00.

Grandin, T. (2000b) My Experiences with Visual Thinking Sensory Problems and Communication Difficulties, Assistant Professor, Colorado State University, Fort Collins, Colorado 80523, USA, accessed 15/07/01, http://www.autism.org/temple/visual.html

Hardy, C. (2000) *ICT for All.* London: David Fulton Publishers.

Herskowitz, V. (2000) 'Computer-based therapy for individuals with autism', *ADVANCE Magazine* (The Nation's Speech-Language and Audiology Weekly), 10 January.

Jordan, R. and Powell, S. (1990) 'Teaching autistic children to think more effectively'. *Communication,* **24** (1) 20–23.

Kaye, A. (ed.) (1991) *Collaborative Learning through Computer Conferencing.* The Najaden Papers. Milton Keynes: Open University/Springer-Verlag.

Longhorn, F. (2000) 'Multisensory education and learners with profound autism', in Powell, S. (ed.), *Helping Children with Autism to Learn.* London: David Fulton Publishers.

Murray, D. K. C. (1997) 'Autism and information technology: therapy with computers', in Powell, S. and Jordan, R., *Autism and Learning.* London: David Fulton Publishers.

The National Curriculum on Line, accessed 09/05/2001, Planning, teaching and assessing the curriculum for pupils with learning difficulties http://www.nc.uk.net/ld/.

Newton, C. and Wilson, D. (1998) *Circles of Friends.* Folens Primary Professional Development. Dunstable: Folens.

Park, C. C. (2001) *Exiting Nirvana: a Daughter's Life with Autism.* London: Aurum Press.

QCA/DfEE (1999) *National Curriculum for England and Wales, Information and Communication Technology.* London: HMSO.

Robinson, B. (1994) 'Word processing and desk-top publishing', in Underfeed, J. (ed.), *Computer Based Learning: Potential into Practice.* London: David Fulton Publishers.

Scrimshaw, P. (1993) 'Cooperative writing with computers', in Scrimshaw, P. (ed.), *Language, Classrooms and Computers.* London: Routledge.

Teacher Training Agency (1998) Draft of the initial teacher training national curriculum for the use of information and communications technology for subject teaching, http://www.teach-tta.gov.uk/ictst.htm, accessed 04/10/98.

Underwood, J. D. M. and Underwood, G. (1990) *Computers and Learning: Helping Children Acquire Thinking Skills*. Oxford: Blackwell.

Williams, D. (1996*) Autism: an Inside-Out Approach*. London: Jessica Kingsley Publishers.

Williams, D. (1998) *Autism and Sensing*. London: Jessica Kingsley Publishers.

Wing, L. (1996) *The Autistic Spectrum: a Guide for Parents and Professionals*. London: Constable.

Index

UNIVERSITY OF WALES COLLEGE NEWPORT
LIBRARY AND LEARNING RESOURCES CAERLEON